German Shepherds

E·H·HART

by E. C. Mansfield Schalk

Chapter on Health and Disease
Approved by William H. Keaton, D.V.M.

t.f.h.

This book originally appeared as Your Pet German Shepherd. It has been updated and enhanced with beautiful color photographs for this new TFH edition.

Cover: Gerard photo of Caesar von Stephanitz, bred by John and Roberta Brejack, and owned by Leon Wilson.

Photos: page 20, Fritz Prenzel; page 59, Isabelle Francais; pages 60 (top) and 61 (top), Sally Anne Thompson; pages 60-61 (top center), Louise van der Meid.

Line drawings by Ernest H. Hart and John R. Quinn.

Distributed in the UNITED STATES by T.F.H. Publications, Inc., 211 West Sylvania Avenue, Neptune City, NJ 07753; in CANADA by H & L Pet Supplies Inc., 27 Kingston Crescent, Kitchener, Ontario N2B 2T6; Rolf C. Hagen Ltd., 3225 Sartelon Street, Montreal 382 Quebec; in ENGLAND by T.F.H. Publications Limited, 4 Kier Park, Ascot, Berkshire SL5 7DS; in AUSTRALIA AND THE SOUTH PACIFIC by T.F.H. (Australia) Pty. Ltd., Box 149, Brookvale 2100 N.S.W., Australia; in NEW ZEALAND by Ross Haines & Son, Ltd., 18 Monmouth Street, Grey Lynn, Auckland 2 New Zealand; in SINGAPORE AND MALAYSIA by MPH Distributors Pte., 71-77 Stamford Road, Singapore 0617; in the PHILIPPINES by Bio-Research, 5 Lippay Street, San Lorenzo Village, Makati Rizal; in SOUTH AFRICA by Multipet Pty. Ltd., 30 Turners Avenue, Durban 4001. Published by T.F.H. Publications Inc., Ltd. the British Crown Colony of Hong Kong.

A trio of handsome German Shepherds.

Contents

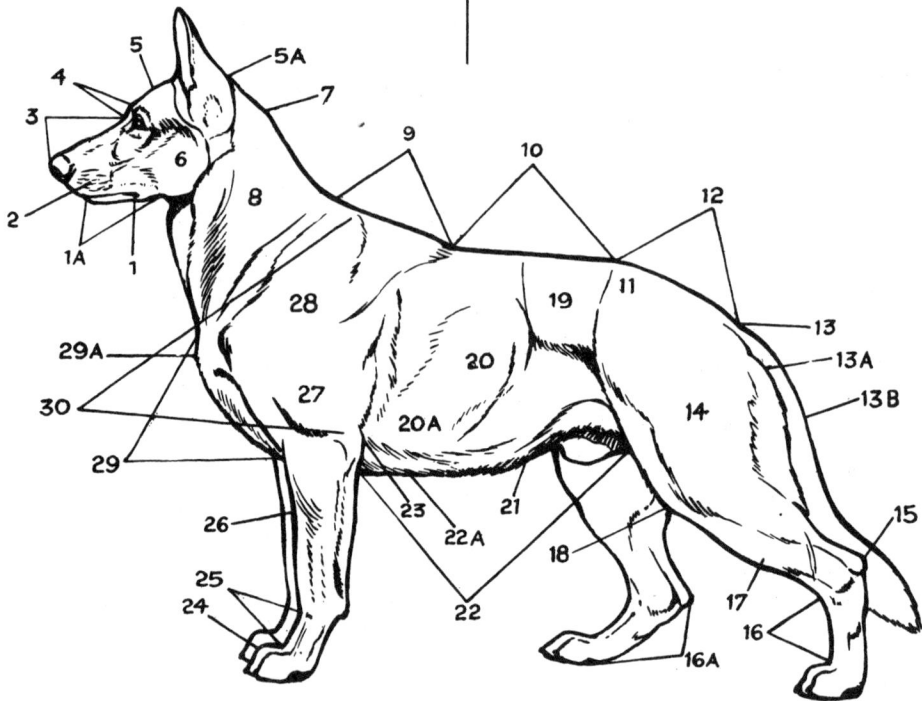

PARTS OF THE GERMAN SHEPHERD DOG

1. Lip corner (flew). 1a. Jaw (lower). 2. Muzzle. 3. Foreface. 4. Stop. 5. Skull. 5a. Occiput. 6. Cheek. 7. Crest (of neck). 8. Neck. 9. Withers. 10. Back. 11. Hip. 12. Croup. 13. Tail set. 13a. Point of Haunch or buttocks. 13b. Tail or stern. 14. Thigh (quarter, haunch). 15. Point of hock. 16. Metatarsus. 16a. Hock. 17. Lower thigh. 18. Point of stifle (knee). 19. Loin. 20. Ribs. 20a. Chest. 21. Abdomen. 22. Bottom line. 23. Elbow. 24. Feet (paws). 25. Pastern. 26. Forearm. 27. Upper arm. 28. Shoulder blade. 29. Forechest. 29a. Prosternum (breastbone). 30. Shoulder.

Introduction

I was having lunch recently with a friend whose business takes him to the far corners of the globe—and he told me he was having a wonderful time with his first German Shepherd dog.

"I thought you were just giving me the old build-up," he said, "but it's true. Shepherds are all over the world. I'm just back from a six-week world trip, and I've seen them everywhere. In Switzerland I saw a platoon of shepherds locating and helping to dig out members of a ski party buried in a snow avalanche. The dogs found every man, although several were buried under twenty feet of snow. All rescued alive! In Helsinki I was ushered into the office of our branch man and there were two Shepherds lying beside his desk. They come every day with him. Then in Lima, our man couldn't meet me at the airport. Detained at a meeting of local Shepherd fanciers!

"And in Calcutta, I called on a classmate one night. Showed him snapshots of my family, our Shepherd sitting right in the front row, of course, so nothing would do but I must steal a peek at his twin sons—already gone to bed. So I did. They were all right, sound asleep in an enormous bed, and right smack between the two kids was a beautiful German Shepherd. My Hindu host explained the outsized bed. Seems that the dog and the children were inseparable, so it had been necessary to get the big bed made in order to accommodate all three!"

And so it goes. For truly the German Shepherd is an international favorite, and he fills many different jobs, too. Sometimes you see him working at his original job of herding cattle or sheep. Sometimes he is a movie star. And because of his fabulous capacity for high specialized training, he is used extensively by state and municipal police in criminal work, tracking and rescue, as well as for the detection of hidden contraband.

His nose and his brain are so keen that he can locate buried metal, concealed narcotics, or illegal distilling operations. He has notable use with the Royal Canadian Mounted Police. Such is his capacity for special training that he is naturally acceptable in the U.S. Armed Services where he is used as sentry dog, communications runner, or as a casualty spotter where he learns to seek out and "report" the presence and location of personnel who are injured and unconscious and might otherwise be left for dead. And in one of his most

5

Introduction

spectacular and most moving roles, we find the Shepherd being the eyes and devoted companion of a blind master.

But for all the varied roles he fills in what we might call "public service to mankind," the German Shepherd's greatest love and starring role is that of being a devoted "family" dog. Here all the wonderful qualities that have made him famous come quietly into full scope. Here he is the children's

German Shepherds are intelligent dogs—and they look it!

playmate, full of fun and face-licking but always with a keen protective "radar" at work so no harm befalls *his* children. Here, as a house dog, he fully uses his almost fanatical love and affection and protective instinct for you, your family and friends. He'll roughouse with you or lie in quiet, dignified adoration. And his keen senses miss nothing. At night he'll hear and investigate strange sounds you can't even hear. Thieves and other evil-doers cannot operate where there's a Shepherd on the job!

Those of us who like dogs usually have a soft spot for *all* dogs. But I can tell you, in all sincerity, if you have never owned a German Shepherd dog, you have missed one of life's greatest pleasures. In fact, you haven't really lived until you and your family have been owned by one!

Origin and History

My daughter and I were visiting a famous zoo, and the one thing on her mind was to see a wolf—a real, live, honest-to-goodness wolf, like the one in "Peter and the Wolf." The wolves were having their regular dens painted, so after a good deal of chasing around we found them in their temporary quarters—all sound asleep of course. "Well, there they are," I said. "Now what do you think of them? Aren't they handsome creatures?" The youngster looked at the animals and then up at me. "Daddy, *no!* Those aren't wolves. They're German Shepherds that got sent to bed early!"

The accurate, scientific facts on the origin of the dog—all dogs, of any breed—prove conclusively that there is no more connection between dogs and wolves than there is between the tiger cat in the grocery store and the tiger in the jungle.

Dogs are descended from a strange animal called *Tomarctus,* which lived way back at the beginning of time. He looked like a combination of dog-raccoon-fox, all scrambled up with a tomcat.

For years, the German Shepherd was referred to as a "Police Dog." There is *no* such breed as "Police Dog." Any dog of any breed is a police dog if it is trained to perform police work. It is not a matter of breed but of training. The American Kennel Club officially terms our breed German Shepherd Dog, a literal translation, word for word, of "Deutsche Schafer Hund," which it is called in the country of its origin. While it is called the "Alsatian" in England, other languages keep to a translation of the original name.

Dog's Place in Man's Life

Due to selective breeding and geographical separation, no race of domestic animals occurs in so many breeds, shapes, sizes, and colors as do our dogs. While many have been produced solely for pets and exhibiting, the oldest breeds, almost without exception, were bred and kept for economic reasons, as well as for protection. Hounds, for example, were first used to procure meat. And there were also the herding dogs which helped in the management and protection of flocks and herds, as well as the owner's person, home, family, and property.

In Germany there was an old, old race of shepherd dogs widely used throughout that and neighboring lands. No one really knew just how old the breed was. It had seemingly always been there. While it varied a good deal as to size, coat, and coloring, still wherever it was found it was readily recognized as a special type.

About the middle of the nineteenth century, this amazing race of shepherd dogs came under the study of one Max von Stephanitz, a cavalry officer and brilliant student of animal genetics.

Horand von Grafrath S.Z. 1—the first German Shepherd Dog to be registered.

Here, he observed, was a race of dogs having great natural beauty coupled with fantastically acute intelligence and senses. These dogs seemed to think, to use judgment entirely apart from anything they had been taught to do. Without directions of any kind, this shepherd dog would seek out a freezing newborn lamb and tenderly pick it up and carry it to his owner. This same dog could destroy or drive off animals much larger than itself if they threatened the flock. The dog knew what to do when sheep strayed into cultivated fields. Without command and entirely of his own volition, this dog would either circle the flock or go straight across their backs to force the wandering ones back into the flock. He knew when to string out the flock to cross a narrow bridge, and he knew when to bunch up the sheep again after crossing. And all this with the barest minimum of training and the most haphazard breeding.

Breeding Standards Set

Captain von Stephanitz resolved on a plan and assembled a group of friends to discuss it with them. Just think, he told them, what could be done. Set a goal in the form of a Standard of Excellence and breed these dogs according to the strictest rules, keeping careful records of what individuals regularly produced what characteristics in their offspring. Breed ever so carefully, only from the best, and keep it up *permanently*. Constantly standardize and improve the physical type of the dog; but,

Temperament and Personality

even more important, further develop and always keep that uncanny brain, that "natural" judgment, those acute senses, always toward the Standard of Excellence. Set up an organization to foster, direct, and record this great project. Do this, he told his friends, and here will be a breed of dogs unequalled!

Roland von Starkenburg, an important early sire.

And so this group drew up the Standard of Excellence and incorporated it into the Verein fur Deutsche Schafer Hunde. Through the work done and continued by this organization, the German Shepherd Dog Club of America, and by breed clubs in other parts of the world, we have the superb, standard-bred German Shepherd Dog as we know him today.

Rich man, poor man, and way stations in between, just ask any owner of a German Shepherd why he has one. Sure, he was probably first attracted to the breed by its great physical beauty. But no matter what language he speaks, or what his choice of words to describe it, you'll hear that the *character* of the German Shepherd is even more wonderful than its appearance.

Character, as the dictionary will tell you, is individuality, personality, qualities, and differences that add up to make a thing unique and distinctive. That is the German Shepherd in your home. Possessor of a brilliant heritage, he is a current edition of the sum total that has made his breed famous the world over.

Devotion to His Family

Probably the German Shepherd's most outstanding characteristic is his devotion and adoration of his human family. It is an unswerving devotion that pervades every moment of the dog's life with you. It is a devotion to you and yours that is almost beyond human understanding in its extent and depth. And this devotion, plus uncanny intelligence, is quite

9

Temperament and Personality

logically coupled with the boundless urge to take care of you, to protect you—no matter what.

Does that sound like so much flowery talk? Well, then consider one instance (and I can give you thousands) of a German Shepherd guiding his sightless master around city streets all day without once indicating or flinching from the acute pain caused by a piece of sharp wire through his paw. Never did the pain deter the dog for one instant from the careful protection of his master from traffic, curbs, steps, and crowds.

Sense of Impending Disaster

Take another instance. Recently, out of hundreds of nominations (and a large percentage were German Shepherds), the National Dog Hero award was given to a German Shepherd. Why?

The dog, then under a year old, had been purchased only a few weeks before the event. He was in the backyard with his owners when all of a sudden he rushed for the back door, tearing at it with all his strength to get into the house. The puzzled owners let the dog in and he raced for the living room, jumped into the playpen, picked up their year-old son by the seat of the pants, rushed him out of the house and dumped him on the grass. He then barked furiously to get his owners to come out there, too. They did, and in split seconds there was a roaring explosion, and instantly the whole house was aflame. The house and contents were gone before the firemen got there, but the family was safe.

This is no piece of fiction. The story was investigated and run by every news and wire service in the country. But how did the dog know that disaster was imminent? The owners didn't know it. There was no warning of sound or smoke. Why did the dog rescue a baby he hardly even knew? Well, that's German Shepherd character!

Suspicion of Strangers

Now somewhere along the line you may have been told that a Shepherd is a "one-man dog," a phrase which means just what it says—a dog that will accept no one but his owner, or who is hostile to all others.

This term does not apply to the German Shepherd. He is not a one-man dog. But while he will be friendly and affectionate with your friends and neighbors whom he knows and sees often, he doesn't like

Exercise and Environment

strangers. Any German Shepherd worth feeding is instantly suspicious of strangers! And, in general, he doesn't wish to be patted by strangers. He wants the strangers to commit themselves first. Are they friends of yours, he wants to know? He'll take his cue from you. If you say it's all right—then it's all right with him, and he'll come around and "make up" to the new people. All of which is a perfectly natural extension of a Shepherd's inborn, inbred protectiveness. But if you don't like this characteristic in a dog, then don't buy a German Shepherd!

And this same protective instinct carries over to your children. He won't like strangers fooling with them. And if he's in your car, he will sharply resent it if anyone tries to get in it, touch it, or take anything out of it. He is not being silly. He's not being mean. He is showing proper Shepherd character.

But the German Shepherd is essentially a happy dog. He enjoys his training, and he trains so easily. He is happy to do what you want. He's happy to be with you and the family. He's happy to lie quietly or rush around and play. He's happy to go for a walk, and he's happy he has you for an owner. In fact, being as smart as he is, he's probably happy he was born a German Shepherd.

The German Shepherd Dog is an all-weather dog, equally at home either in the tropics or in areas of almost constant snow and low temperatures. He adapts himself to any kind of adequate housing in any climate, with no special consideration as far as weather is concerned. In a permanently cold climate or in sections with very cold winters, nature equips him accordingly. On parting the hair of the coat, you will see a dense undercoat of soft, fine hair, which acts as insulation against cold and dampness. Whereas this undercoat usually grows in the early fall in cold climates, the Shepherd in the tropics may grow one at the usual time, but it will be less heavy. In successive years the undercoat will grow less, and finally stops growing.

Outdoor or Indoor Dog

The Shepherd, in cold climates, may be kept with perfect safety in an outside, unheated kennel or building, provided he is fully protected from wind, drafts, and dampness. But if this is to be his life, he must be kept mainly in the cold. He must not be allowed to come into a heated atmosphere for long periods of time and then be

Exercise and Environment

put outside. In other words, if he is primarily an outside dog, he must be kept that way.

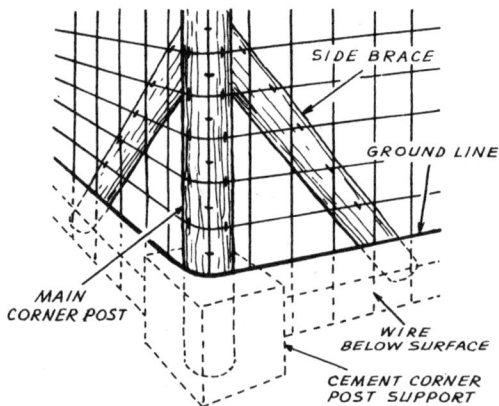

Cedar post run corner.

In extremely hot weather, see to it that he has a cool, shady place to rest during the hottest part of the day. And most important, see to it that he has an adequate supply of clean, fresh water readily available at all times. A galvanized pail hung from a hook is ideal if changed often. Be sure, in placing the hook, that the pail is not too high for the dog to reach the last drop of water in the bottom. This is a good setup, however, since young dogs seem to love to tip over water pails and make giant mud puddles.

If there is any place to swim in fresh water, encourage your dog to do it. It is both cooling and good exercise. But for this and other exercise, try to limit it to early morning or evening in very hot weather. In general, I believe it is best not to allow a dog to swim in salt water. Although many dogs are not adversely affected, the combination of salt water and sand can result in disorders of the skin and coat.

Finished house.

Never Clip His Coat

And speaking of coats, good brushing in hot weather is just as important as at any other time. But

Exercise and Environment

don't under any circumstance allow yourself to be talked into having your Shepherd clipped or shaved "to make him more comfortable." This is the worst possible thing to do. His coat was put there as protection from direct rays of the sun and for protection against insects, rough ground, and such. Cut off his coat and your dog will probably come down with every skin trouble in the book—and Shepherds almost never have skin troubles. Leave his coat on him!

City or Country Dog

"Oh I'd love to have a German Shepherd, but I can't. I live in the city in an apartment." This is usually the remark of a person who "just adores" dogs—as long as they belong to somebody else and he isn't concerned with taking proper care of them.

Forget all the nonsense you ever heard about a Shepherd requiring a hundred acres in the country. He doesn't. I tell you, and I have done it for years, you can keep a full-grown Shepherd in a small apartment, and he will enjoy perfect physical and mental health. He is just as happy in the city as he is in the country, providing you are there.

It isn't easy to keep a dog in the city—granted, but it can be done with great success. With a young puppy, it requires eight to ten trips to the sidewalk each day. And see to it that you start at once to train your dog to use the gutter, *not* the sidewalk. He'll learn this in two or three days easily. Just guide him into the gutter and hold him there with the leash until he is finished. Then praise him for being a good dog. Be sure to clean up after your dog, as this is required in most places in the United States. In addition, he should have some leash-walking, say two or three trips around the block.

As your Shepherd matures, the "constitutionals" to the gutter will be cut to two or three a day, in addition to at least an hour, morning and night, of good, brisk leash-walking. If the neighborhood permits, chasing and retrieving a stick or ball is wonderful exercise, as is running and playing with another dog. And while a lot of people may disagree sharply with me on this point, I have found that proper feeding, grooming, and the above exercise is perfectly adequate for a Shepherd to thrive on. Of course, the more exercise the merrier. If you really want a German Shepherd, even though you

Your New Puppy

live in an apartment, you can certainly have one. Just do what has to be done for the dog without thinking of it as a chore. The exercising will be good for you, too. You'll come to enjoy it!

Of course in the suburbs or the country, life is simpler. Your dog can simply go outside into a fenced-in yard.

Taking your puppy for regular walks can be more than a pleasant experience—it is essential for good muscle tone and bone development.

J. R. Quinn

You have chosen to own a German Shepherd puppy. You have chosen it very carefully over all other breeds. So before you ever get that puppy home, you will have prepared for its arrival by reading everything you can get your hands on having to do with the management of dogs and puppies. True, you will run into many conflicting opinions, but at least you will not be starting "blind." Read, study, digest. Talk over your plans with your veterinarian, other "dog people," and the seller of your puppy.

When you get your puppy, you will find that your reading and study are far from finished. You've just scratched the surface in your plan to provide the greatest possible comfort and health of your Shepherd puppy, and, by the same token, assure yourself of the greatest possible enjoyment of this wonderful creature. You must be ready for the puppy mentally as well as in the physical requirements.

The First Day and Night

When your puppy arrives in your home, put him down on the floor and never again pick him up, except when it is absolutely necessary. He

14

Your New Puppy

is a dog, a real dog, and must not be lugged around like a rag doll. handle him as little as possible, and permit no one to pick him up and baby him. To repeat, *put your puppy on the floor or the ground and let him stay there except when it may be necessary to do otherwise.*

Quite possibly your puppy will be afraid for a while in his new surroundings, without his mother and littermates. Comfort him and reassure him, but don't console him. Don't give him the "oh-you-poor-ittsy-bitsy-puppy" treatment. Be calm, friendly, and reassuring. Encourage him to walk around and sniff over his new home. If it's dark, put on the lights. Let him roam for a few minutes while you and everybody else concerned sit quietly or go about your routine business. Let the puppy come back to you.

For his first night with you, I recommend that he be put where he is to sleep every night—say the kitchen, since its floor can easily be swabbed. Let him explore the kitchen to his heart's content; close doors to confine him there. Prepare his food and feed him lightly the first night. Give him a pan with some water in it—not a lot, since most puppies will try to drink the whole pan dry. Give him an old coat or a shirt to lie on. Since a coat or shirt will be strong in human scent, he will pick it out to lie on, thus furthering his feeling of security in the room where he has just been fed.

Housebreaking Helps

Now, sooner or later—mostly sooner—your new puppy is going to "puddle" on the floor. First take a newspaper and lay it on the puddle until the urine is soaked up onto the paper. *Save this paper.* Now take a cloth with soap and water, wipe up the floor and dry it well. Then take the wet paper and place it on a fairly large square of newspapers in a convenient corner. When cleaning up, always keep a piece of wet paper on top of the others. Every time he wants to "squat," he will seek out this spot and use the papers. (This routine is rarely necessary for more than three days.) Now leave your puppy for the night. Quite probably he will cry and howl a bit; some are more stubborn than others on this matter. But let him stay alone for the night. This may seem harsh treatment, but in my opinion and experience, it is the best procedure in the long run. Just let him cry; he will weary of it sooner or later.

Your New Puppy

Beat Him to the Draw

Puppies, like human infants, wake up at the crack of dawn. So bright and early, your first job is to take him outdoors for a "business trip." Try to keep him out until he has relieved himself. Then give him his first meal of the day, after which you take him out again. Puppies usually want to relieve themselves first thing in the morning, last thing at night, after each feeding, and after each nap. To cut down on "mistakes," take him out often for the first few days, until he learns what he is going out for—and keep him near his newspapers. Caution: do not force him to rely too much on the newspapers or he will get to the point where he will stay out for hours without doing and then rush to the paprs when he at last is brought indoors.

Housebreaking is a simple thing if done properly. I have never seen a Shepherd puppy that took more than three days on my procedure. Just cooperate with the inevitable! Anticipate his need before he does. And for the first few mistakes, say nothing to him—especially the first 24 hours. Then, when he misbehaves, point to the error and quietly but firmly say "No" or "Pfui" (as in "fooey"). Make it decisive. He must know he has done wrong, but he must *not* be scared to death. And under no circumstance must he be slapped, yelled at, or stamped at. Just a brisk "Pfui" or "no." Work things in such a way that he doesn't get a chance to misbehave.

Collar and Leash Training

Now as to general management, immediately put on him a small leather collar and have a leash to go with it. He probably won't notice the collar at all, but if he does, and seems to fight it, let him fight it and

The intelligent expression of the German Shepherd is greatly enhanced by ears that are carried erect. p. 17; Good representatives of the German Shepherd breed are easy to recognize. p. 18-19; German Shepherds come in a variety of shades. All colors except white are acceptable for show dogs. p. 20-21; Typical markings of German Shepherds (head and body) are well represented in these pictures. p. 22-23; The outer coat of a German Shepherd is dense and consists of harsh straight hair. p. 24.

Your New Puppy

pay no attention. He'll get used to it quickly. Leave it on all the time. Whenever he goes outside, snap a leash onto the collar. City or country, always take your dog out with collar and leash. This is his first taste of discipline. And as I have said before, discipline is not punishment—it is training!

As you will see later, all training is done on the leash. He may buck and plunge a bit at first, finding himself unable to run around at will. Hold the leash firmly, but let it "give" a lot for the first few days. Do not start him off with the chain collar. Such a collar is ideal, but it is painful and even dangerous on a young puppy. Gradually teach him to walk quietly on the leash, always on your left side. Hold the leash in such a way to prevent him from running ahead of you or crossing your path. By all means, start his leash and collar work as soon as you get him. Don't start his formal training until he is five or six months old, or maybe a little older, depending on the dog himself. Meanwhile, he is learning what "No" means, and he is learning to come when called. Always speak his name first, followed by the command "Come." And make it a command, but slap your knees to encourage him at first. Study your training

book now, even though you won't start regular training for months.

Most German Shepherds, particularly young ones, do not like strangers. By instinct, they distrust strangers. This distrust is much stronger in a puppy than in an adult dog that has "been around." Encourage your Shepherd puppy to be friendly with everyone. If he is timid with strangers, have them feed him bits of something he especially likes to eat. Thus you encourage the puppy to go up to anybody. This training will not in any way prevent him from being a good watchdog on maturity. But arrange things so that the puppy goes to the stranger, not the other way around. In fact, have your guests ignore the puppy. Let him go to them—always. Let them pat him casually, and no more. No roughhousing or making a great fuss.

Riding in the Car

Start your puppy off right in the car. He will probably have to be boosted in the first few times. Let him sit on the floor. Take him only on short trips for awhile. If the excitement or motion of riding makes him sick, he will begin to drool heavily. When you see this, stop the car and take him out. Let him walk around on the leash a bit—say five or ten minutes. Then put him back in the car and start off again. Go for short trips only, for several weeks, and make the trips frequent. The younger the puppy, usually the sooner he learns to like driving and the less he is concerned with it.

Take your puppy everywhere—streets, stores—everywhere. Do it in easy stages, but get him accustomed to all sorts of strange sights, sounds, and smells. Thus, when he is mature, he will go anywhere with perfect poise.

Encourage him, too, to stand quietly and be patted by strangers. Be careful that he doesn't learn to dislike children, as sometimes happens with dogs of all breeds, because of rough handling on the part of the children. Let one or two children take him for a walk on his leash once in a while. Let them feed him some special treat as they take him out.

Introducing New Situations

In general, either lead your Shepherd or encourage him to take the initiative in all new situations. Don't ever "push" him into them. You will get nowhere and may end up spoiling the dog.

With you and your family, observe the same procedures. Let the dog make the move. Encourage him to sit or lie quietly with the family. Let the dog develop into a sensible, normal dog. Don't fuss with him constantly. And no matter how cute he is, don't pick him up. Keep him off the furniture.

When I say don't make a fuss over him, do not misunderstand me. I would be the last person in the world to encourage you to bring up your dog in a harsh, strict manner. A Shepherd has a limitless reservoir of love and affection and devotion for those he knows and loves. It is a Shepherd characteristic to be that way. Sure, play with him. Sure, roughhouse with him, but don't make an addlepated ninny out of him by constantly fooling or talking with him. If there is anything worse than a spoiled child, it's a spoiled dog. Both are a pain in the neck to all concerned. So bring up your Shepherd to be a friendly, well-mannered, happy, healthy dog. If he doesn't "get around," how can he know how to act under all circumstances? So take him around. Start his training early.

Feeding

Now let's talk about feeding your German Shepherd, a subject so simple that it's amazing there is so much nonsense and misunderstanding about it. Is it expensive to feed a German Shepherd? No, it is not! You can feed your Shepherd economically and keep him in perfect shape the year round, or you can feed him expensively. He'll thrive either way, and let's see why this is true.

First of all, remember a dog is a dog, even if he is a German Shepherd! Dogs do not have a high degree of selectivity in their food, and unless you spoil them with great variety (and possibly turn them into poor, "picky" eaters) they will eat almost anything that they become accustomed to. I have seen many dogs that flatly refuse to eat nice, fresh beef. They picked around it and ate everything else. But meat—bah! Why? They weren't accustomed to it! They were hounds. They'd eat rabbit fast enough, but they refused beef because they weren't used to it.

Variety Not Necessary

My advice to you is to forget all about human preferences and don't give a thought to variety. Choose the right diet for your dog and feed it to him day after day, year after year, winter and summer. But what is the right diet for your German Shepherd?

There are almost as many right diets as there are dog experts. I can only tell you what I think is right, the diet that has been right for my dogs and their litters, year after year.

Rickets in a German Shepherd puppy, the result of a dietary deficiency.

27

Feeding

Hundreds of thousands of dollars have been spent in canine nutrition research. The results are pretty conclusive, so you needn't go into a lot of experimenting with trials of this and that every other week. Research has proven just what your dog needs to eat and keep healthy.

Dry-Type Dog Food

My preference for my own dogs, and I heartily recommend it to you, is a dry type of food, either meal or kibble form, for your dog's basic diet. There are several of these of excellent quality, manufactured by reliable concerns, research tested, and nationally advertised. They are inexpensive, highly satisfactory, and easily available in stores everywhere in containers of five to fifty pounds. Larger amounts cost less per pound, usually.

If you have a choice of brands, it is usually safer to choose the better-known one, but even so, carefully read the analysis on the package. Do not choose any food in which the protein level is less than 25 per cent, and be sure that this protein comes from both animal *and* vegetable sources. The good dog foods have meat meal, fish meal, liver, and such, plus protein from

alfalfa and soy beans, as well as some dried milk product. Note the vitamin content carefully. See that they are all there in good proportions; and be especially certain that the food contains properly high levels of vitamins A and D, two of the most perishable and important ones. Note the B complex level, but don't worry about carbohydrate and mineral levels. These substances are plentiful and cheap and not likely to be lacking in a good brand.

Having chosen a really good food, feed it to your Shepherd as the manufacturer directs. And once you've started, stick to it. Never change if you can possibly help it. A switch from one meal or kibble-type food can usually be made without too much upset; however, a change will almost invariably give you (and the dog) some trouble.

Fat Important; Meat Optional

While the better dog foods are complete in themselves in every respect, there is one item to add to the food, and that is *fat*—any kind of melted animal fat. It can be lard, bacon, or ham fat or from beef, lamb, pork or poultry. A grown dog should have at least three tablespoons of melted fat added to one feeding a day. If you feed your dog morning and night, give him half that amount in each feeding.

The addition of meat to this basic ration is optional. There is a sufficient amount of everything your dog needs already in the food. I have raised fat, heavy-boned litters on this type of food, adding nothing extra but milk. You may add any meat you wish, say a half to a quarter of a pound. In adding meat, the glandular meats are best, such as kidneys, pork liver, and veal or beef heart. They are all cheap to buy and are far higher sources of protein than the usual muscle meat we humans insist on. Cook these meats slightly or feed them raw. Liver and kidney should be cooked a little and fed sparingly since they are laxative to some dogs. Heart is ideal, raw or cooked. Or you can feed horsemeat, beef, lamb, ocean fish well cooked, and pork. Yes, even pork, although for some reason this fine meat has been supposed to be no good for dogs.

When Supplements Are Needed

Now what about supplements of various kinds, mineral and vitamin, or the various oils? They are all right to add to your Shepherd's food. However, if you are feeding your dog a correct diet, and this is easy to do, it is my confirmed opionion that no supplements are necessary unless your dog has been improperly fed, has been sick, or is having puppies. Vitamins and minerals are naturally present in all foods, and to ensure against any loss through processing, they are added in concentrated form to the dog food you use. Except on the advice of your veterinarian, extra and added amounts of vitamins can prove harmful to your dog! The same risk goes with minerals.

When and how much food to give your dog? As to when, except in the instance of puppies which we'll take up later, suit yourself. You may, as I have said, feed two meals per day, or the same amount in one single feeding, either morning or night. As to how to prepare the food and how much to give, it is generally best to follow the directions on the food package. Your own dog may want a little more or a little less.

All Dogs Need to Chew

Puppies and young dogs need something with resistance to chew on while their teeth and jaws are

Feeding

developing—for cutting the puppy teeth, to induce growth of the permanent teeth under the puppy teeth, to assist in getting rid of the puppy teeth at the proper time, to help the permanent teeth through the gums, to assure normal jaw development and to settle the permanent teeth solidly in the jaws.

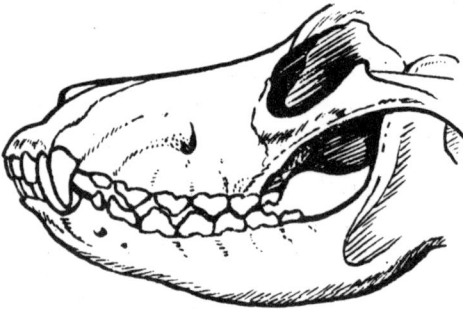

Side view of correct scissors bite.

The adult dog's desire to chew stems from the instinct for tooth cleaning, gum massage and jaw exercise—plus the need for an outlet for periodic doggie tensions.

Dental caries as it affects the teeth of humans is virtually unknown in dogs—but tartar accumulates on the teeth of dogs, particularly at the gum line, more rapidly than on the teeth of humans. These accumulations, if not removed, bring irritation, and then infection which erodes the tooth enamel and ultimately destroys the teeth at the roots. Most chewing by adult dogs is an effort to do something about this problem for themselves.

Tooth and jaw development will normally continue until the dog is more than a year old—but sometimes much longer, depending upon the breed, chewing exercise, the rate at which calcium can be utilized and many other factors, known and unknown, which affect the development of individual dogs. Diseases, like distemper for example, may sometimes arrest development of the teeth and jaws, which may resume months, or even years later.

This is why dogs, especially puppies and young dogs, will often destroy property worth hundreds of dollars, when their chewing instinct is not diverted from their owner's possessions, particularly during the widely varying critical period for young dogs.

Saving your possessions from destruction, assuring proper development of teeth and jaws, providing for 'interim' tooth cleaning and gum massage, and channeling doggie tensions into a non-destructive outlet are, therefore, all dependent upon the dog having something suitable for chewing

Feeding

readily available when his instinct tells him to chew. If your purposes, and those of your dog, are to be accomplished, what you provide for chewing must be desirable from the doggie viewpoint, have the necessary functional qualities, and above all, be safe for your dog.

Frontal view of correct scissors bite.

It is very important that dogs not be permitted to chew on anything they can break, or indigestible things from which they can bite sizeable chunks. Sharp pieces, from such as a bone which can be broken by a dog, may pierce the intestine wall and kill. Indigestible things which can be bitten off in chunks, such as toys made of rubber compound or cheap plastic, may cause an intestinal stoppage, if not regurgitated—to bring painful death, unless surgery is promptly performed.

Strong natural bones, such as 4 to 8 inch lengths of round shin bone from mature beef—either the kind you can get from your butcher or one of the variety available commercially in pet stores—may serve your dog's teething needs, if his mouth is large enough to handle them effectively.

You may be tempted to give your puppy a smaller bone and he may not be able to break it when you do—but puppies grow rapidly and the power of their jaws constantly increases until maturity. This means that a growing dog may break one of the smaller bones at any time, swallow the pieces and die painfully before you realize what is wrong.

Many people make the mistake of thinking of their dog's teeth in terms of the teeth of the wild carnivores or those of the dog in antiquity. The teeth of the wild carnivorous animals, and the teeth found in the fossils of the dog-like creatures of antiquity, have far thicker and stronger enamel than those of our contemporary dogs.

All hard natural bones are highly abrasive. If your dog is an avid chewer, natural bones may wear away his teeth prematurely; hence, they then should be taken away from your dog when the teething purposes have been served. The

Feeding

badly worn, and usually painful, teeth of many mature dogs can be traced to excessive chewing on natural bones.

Contrary to popular belief, knuckle bones which can be chewed up and swallowed by the dog provide little, if any, useable calcium or other nutriment. They do, however, disturb the digestion of most dogs and cause them to vomit the nourishing food they need.

An old leather shoe is another popular answer to the chewing need—but be very sure that the rubber heel, all nails, and other metal parts such as lace grommets, metal arches, etc., have been removed. Be especially careful to get all of the nails. A chunk of rubber heel can cause an intestinal stoppage. If it has a nail in it, the intestine wall may be pierced or torn. Then there is, of course, always the hazard that your dog may fail to differentiate between his shoe and yours, and eat up a good pair while you're not looking.

Dried rawhide products of various types, shapes, sizes and prices are available on the market and have become quite popular. However, they don't serve the primary chewing functions very well; they are a bit messy when wet from mouthing, and most dogs chew them up rather rapidly—but they have been considered safe for dogs until recently. Now, more and more incidents of death, and near death, by strangulation have been reported to be the result of partially swallowed chunks of rawhide

---

Traditional playthings are not necessarily safe playthings. Nails and the rubber heel of a shoe, for example, could cause problems if ingested.

J. R. Quinn

Feeding

swelling in the throat. More recently, some veterinarians have been attributing cases of acute constipation to large pieces of incompletely digested rawhide in the intestine.

The nylon bones, especially those with natural meat and bone fractions added, are probably the most complete, safe and economical answer to the chewing need. Dogs cannot break them or bite off sizeable chunks; hence, they are

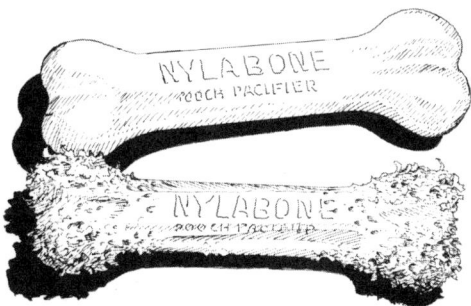

The upper Nylabone has not yet been chewed; the lower Nylabone shows normal signs of wear.

completely safe—and being longer lasting than other things offered for the purpose, they are economical.

Hard chewing raises little bristle-like projections on the surface of the nylon bones—to provide effective interim tooth cleaning and vigorous gum massage, much in the same way your toothbrush does it for you. The little projections are raked off and swallowed in the form of thin shavings—but the chemistry of the nylon is such that they break down in the stomach fluids and pass through without effect.

The toughness of the nylon provides the strong chewing resistance needed for important jaw exercise and effective help for the teething functions—but there is no tooth wear because nylon is non-abrasive. Being inert, nylon does not support the growth of microorganisms —and it can be washed in soap and water, or it can be sterilized by boiling or in an autoclave.

Nylabone® is highly recommended by veterinarians as a safe, healthy nylon bone that can't splinter or chip. Instead, Nylabone is frizzled by the dog's chewing action, creating a toothbrush-like surface that cleanses the teeth and massages the gums. Nylabone® and Nylaball® , the only chew products made of flavor-impregnated solid nylon, are available in your local pet shop.

Nothing, however, substitutes for periodic professional attention to your dog's teeth and gums, not any more than your toothbrush can do that for you. Have your dog's teeth cleaned by your veterinarian at least once a year, twice a year is better—and he will be healthier, happier and far more pleasant to live with.

Training

Because of the breed's inherited capacity for training, the German Shepherd puppy in your home is legitimate heir to a glorious history of service and pleasure to mankind. You owe proper training to your Shepherd. The right and privilege of being trained is his birthright, and no breed of dog trains more readily or more surely than the Shepherd.

Now whether your Shepherd is going to be a handsome, well-mannered housedog and companion, a dog used for herding stock or tracking lost persons, or whatever

1. Limited choke. 2. Pliable leash, 6 feet long. 3. Chain choke collar. 4. Wooden dumbbell. 5. Long leash.

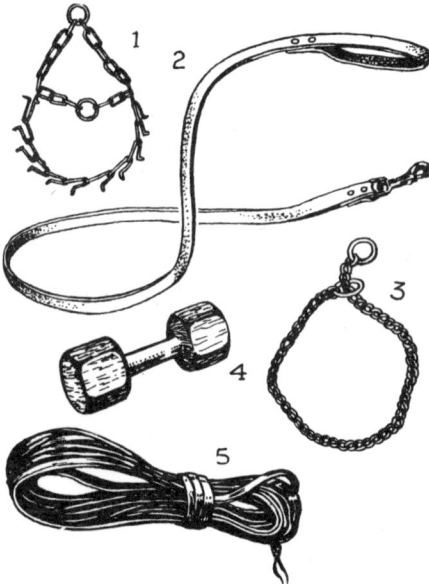

possible use he may be put to, the basic training is always the same. Police dog, army dog, guide dog for the blind, all must start with basic obedience—or what might be called "manners training."

Your dog must come instantly when called, and obey the "sit" or "down" command just as fast; he must walk quietly at "heel," whether on or off the lead. He must be mannerly and polite wherever he goes; he must be polite to strangers on the street and in stores. He must be orderly in the presence of other dogs. He must not bark at children on roller skates, motorcycles, or domestic animals. And he must be restrained from chasing cats. It is not a dog's inalienable right to chase cats, and he must be reprimanded for it.

Send to Professional Trainer

How do you go about this training? Well, it's a very simple procedure, pretty well standardized by now. First, if you can afford the extra expense, you may send your dog to a professional trainer, where in 30 to 60 days he will learn how to be "a good dog." If you enlist the services of a good professional trainer, follow his advice about when to come to see the dog. No, he won't forget you, but too-frequent visits at the wrong time may slow down his training progress. And in using a "pro" trainer you will have to go for some training, too, after the trainer feels your dog is ready to go home. You will have to learn how your dog works and just what to expect of him and how to use what the dog has learned after he is home.

Join Obedience Training Class

Another way to train your dog (I think this is the best of the three) is to join an obedience training class right in your own community. There is such a group in nearly every community nowadays. Here you will be working with a group of people who are also just starting out. You will actually be training your own dog, since all work is done under the direction of a head trainer who will make suggestions to you and also tell you when and how to correct your dog's errors. Then, too, working with such a group, your dog will learn to get along with other dogs. And, what is more important, he will learn to do exactly what he is told to do, no matter how much confusion there is

around him, or how great the temptation to go his own way.

Write to the American Kennel Club for the location of a training club or class in your locality. Sign up. Go to it regularly—every session! Go early and leave late! Both you and your dog will benefit tremendously.

Training for the show requires patience and knowledge.

Train Him By The Book

The third way of training your dog is by the book. Yes, you can do it this way and do a good job of it too. If you can read and if you're smarter than the dog, you'll do a good job. But in using the book method, select a book, buy it, study it carefully; then study it some more, until the procedures are almost second nature to you. *Then* start your training. But stay with the book and its advice and exercises. Don't start in and then make up a few rules of your own. If you don't follow the book, you'll get into jams you can't get out of by yourself. If, after a few hours of short training session your dog is still not working as he should, get back to the book for a study session, because it's *your* fault, not the dog's! The procedures of dog training have been so well systematized that it must be your fault, since literally thousands of fine German Shepherds have been trained by the book.

After your Shepherd is "letter perfect" under all conditions, then if you wish, go on to advanced training and trick work. Teach him to track. You never know when a dog with a trained nose can be of great service to your community or to you personally.

Forget Attack Training

Now a word of warning. I have had many inquiries from well-intentioned amateur trainers who want to teach their Shepherds attack and protection work. True, the Shepherd has the brain to do what

it is told and to stop when so told, but attack and protection training is *strictly* for experienced trainers of many years' practice. Such a dog, properly trained, is *not* a vicious or unpredictable dog, but he should *never* be owned or kept by a private individual—not ever. Such a dog with the average owner is a highly dangerous weapon. He belongs in military, police, or security forces *only*—never in private hands. You don't need attack or protection training in your dog, and, in my opinion, you have no right to have a dog so trained.

Your Shepherd will love his obedience training, and you'll burst with pride at the finished product! Your dog will enjoy life even more, and you'll enjoy your dog more. And remember—you *owe* good training to your German Shepherd!

Grooming

Your German Shepherd probably requires less grooming than any other breed of dog. Here again, you can do what is necessary in two minutes, or if you choose, you can make a lengthy theatrical production out of it. Actually, the job is simple and the necessary tools and supplies are few, inexpensive and easy to use.

Bathing Rarely Necessary

Let's begin with the subject of washing your Shepherd. This is the simplest problem of all to solve. Just *don't* wash him.

Your dog's coat is so constructed that it is virtually impossible to get dirty. Certainly he can get mud on himself, or paint, or grease. In any case, the soiling is right on the surface of the coat. For mud, the easiest thing to do is squirt a hose on him, or else let the mud dry and get it off with good, hard brushing. For tar, paint, oil, and such, use gasoline, ether, turpentine, or kerosene—a little on a cloth—and dab the soiled area with it. If it's a large area, follow the same procedure and then wash him in mild soap and warm water, since the cleaning fluid you have used will surely irritate his skin. Rinse him well after using any type of fluid, so that he does not lick off a lethal substance.

Surface dirt, in general, may be removed by rubbing the dog with an old rough towel wrung out in hot water. Follow this with a dry rub and brushing. If it should be necessary to wash your dog, take proper care in drying him off, especially in the winter.

In the event your dog runs afoul of a skunk (and I do mean afoul) get him to where you can pour lots of water on him. Since "skunk juice" is oily, water tends to float a good deal of it off. Following the repeated water treatment, soap and rinse him several times. All the smell will have to wear off!

Keep Him Well Brushed

For grooming equipment, your Shepherd mostly needs a large, stiff brush. A horse brush is ideal. Apply it vigorously, brushing first from tail to head, then head to tail. Then take a fairly coarse metal comb and comb out the brush of his tail. And that's it.

I have heard people complain that sometimes dogs get to smelling "doggy." Just what that means, I wouldn't know. But if you think your dog smells "doggy," invest in some of the good "dry bath"

Grooming

liquids or sprays that are on the market. They do help to groom the coat and usually have a pleasant, woodsy smell. Of course, follow the directions for use carefully. If you are fussy, you might follow this procedure once a week. But again, don't wash him. Washing should, in my opinion, be avoided. Undoubtedly it upsets the ideal condition of a normal, healthy skin and coat.

Trim Nails Regularly

Now about toenails. Most dogs need their nails cut every two or three months. Your veterinarian might do this for you, but he is a busy medical man, and besides, you should learn to do it yourself. It's very easy.

Equip yourself with a dog's nail cutter that looks a little like a ticket punch. There is a hole in the metal where the actual punch would be. This you hold over the tip of the nail and with a quick, hard squeeze on the handles, a flat blade shoots across the tip of the nail, cutting it off. Avoid the pincer or scissors type nail cutters. They pinch and hurt, and you'll have quite a struggle to complete the job.

Study your dog's nails carefully. Never allow them to get long, because, aside from any other

reason, long nails will ruin his feet. In cutting the nails, work in a strong light with the dog lying flat on his side. Cut off just the tip of the nail for the first few times, until you are skillful at it. Do all four feet, of course, and use care not to cut into the quick. If you do, it may bleed a little, but it usually doesn't require any treatment. If it bleeds a lot, hold some styptic powder against the nail until the bleeding stops. Try to keep the nails cut back so they extend only a little beyond the line of the paw.

By removing dead hair, dust, and skin in the daily grooming, you keep your Shepherd's coat glossy and his appearance neat.

J.R. Quihn

Showing

Watch For Parasites

Occasionally it may happen that your Shepherd will pick up fleas (of course, from that mutt next door!), but there is no cause for alarm. They can be eliminated just as fast as they are picked up. Rarely will an infestation be heavy enough to require a washing with flea soap. One of the powders that are dusted into the coat will usually suffice. Follow the package directions carefully.

Dogs rarely pick up lice. However, in the event your dog does, consult your veterinarian. Or, if you live in an area where there is a tick season, it is a matter of going over your dog at least every two days, literally with a fine-tooth comb, to locate and remove small ticks or larger ones that have not yet attached themselves to the dog's skin. Large ticks that have already burrowed into the skin should be anesthetized with rubbing alcohol and then removed with tweezers and the slight wounds dabbed with some mild antiseptic. Ticks are hard to destroy; it's best to burn them.

Groom your dog as often as possible, once a day or twice a week if possible, but always remember that the health of your dog's skin and coat comes from the inside— from correct feeding.

A show dog is a comparatively rare thing. He is one out of several litters of puppies. He happens to be born with a degree of physical perfection that closely approximates the standard by which the breed is judged in the show ring. Such a dog should, on maturity, be able to win or approach his championship in good, fast company at the larger

The ideal German Shepherd male.

shows. Upon finishing his championship, he is apt to be highly desirable as a breeding animal. As a proven stud, he will automatically command a high price for service.

Showing dogs is a lot of fun—yes, but it is a highly competitive sport. While all the experts were once beginners, the odds are against a novice. You will be showing against

Showing

experienced handlers, both pro and amateur, often people who have devoted a lifetime to breeding, picking the right ones, and then showing those dogs through to their championships. Moreover, the most perfect dog ever born has faults, and in your hands the faults will be far more evident than with the experienced handler who knows how to minimize his dog's faults. These are but a few points on the sad side of the picture.

The experienced handler, as I say, was not born knowing the ropes. He learned—*and so can you!* You can if you will put in the same time, study and keen observation that he did. But it will take time!

Key to Success

First, search for a truly fine show prospect. Take the puppy home, raise him by the book, and as carefully as you know how, give him every chance to mature into the dog hoped for. My advice is to keep your dog out of big shows, even Puppy Classes, until he is mature. Maturity in the male is roughly two years; with the female, fourteen months or so. When he is approaching maturity, break him in at match shows (more on these

later), and with this experience for the dog and you, then go gunning for the big wins at the big shows.

Next step, read the standard by which the Shepherd is judged. Study it until you know it by heart. Having done this, and while your puppy is at home (where he should be) growing into a fine normal, healthy dog, go to every dog show you can possibly reach. Sit at the ringside and watch Shepherd judging. Keep your ears and eyes open. Do your own judging, holding each of those dogs against the standard, which you now know by heart.

In your evaluations, don't start off looking for faults. Look for the virtues—the best qualities. How does a given dog shape up against the standard? Having looked for and noted the virtues, then note the faults and see what prevents a given dog from standing correctly or moving well. Weigh these faults against the virtues, since, ideally, every feature of the dog should contribute to the harmonious whole dog.

"Ringside Judging"

It's a good practice to make notes on each dog, always holding the dog against the standard. In "ringside judging," forget your personal

Gerard '82

Dogs intended for the show ring must learn how to pose properly.

preference for this or that feature. What does the standard say about it? Watch carefully as the judge places the dogs in a given class. It is difficult from the ringside always to see why number one was placed over the second dog. Try to follow the judge's reasoning. Later try to talk with the judge after he is finished. Ask him questions as to why he placed certain dogs and not others. Listen while the judge explains his placings, and, I'll say right here, any judge worthy of his license should be able to give reasons.

When you're not at the ringside, talk with the fanciers and breeders where the dogs are benched. Don't be afraid to ask opinions or say that you don't know. You have a lot of listening to do, and it will help you a great deal and speed up your personal progress if you are a good listener.

Join The National Club

You will find it worthwhile to join the German Shepherd Dog Club of America and to subscribe to its magazine. From the national club, you will learn the location of an approved regional club near you.

Now, when your young Shepherd is eight to ten months old, find out the dates of A.K.C. match shows in your section of the country. These differ from regular shows only in that no championship points are given. These shows are especially designed to launch young dogs (and young handlers) on a show career.

Enter The Match Shows

With the ring deportment you have watched at big shows firmly in mind and practice, enter your dog in as many match shows as you can. When in the ring, you have two jobs. One is to see to it that your dog is always being seen to best advantage. The other job is to keep your eye on the judge to see what he may want you to do next. Watch only the judge and your dog. Be quick and be alert; do exactly as the judge directs. Don't speak to him except to answer his questions. If he does something you don't like, don't say so. And don't irritate the judge (and everybody else) by constantly talking and fussing with your dog.

In moving about the ring, remember to keep clear of dogs beside you or in front of you. It is my advice to you *not* to show your Shepherd in a regular point show until he is at least close to maturity and after both you and he have had time to perfect ring manners and poise in the match shows.

Showing

Pre-Show Grooming

Now, for a few grooming pointers before entering the show ring. We have noted that the Shepherd is a completely natural dog and, therefore, requires little if any pre-show grooming. There are, however, a few simple things you can do to enhance the appearance of your Shepherd.

First, be sure his nails are well cut back, and his fur is as good and clean as normal brushing will keep it. On the day of the show, take an ordinary face cloth and wring it out in hot water and wipe out the inside of your Shepherd's ears, especially the hairless part near the base of the ear. Do it gently and see to it that no water runs to the inner ear. Now rinse out the cloth and wipe the eyes and nose carefully.

Put your horse brush into vigorous action. Brush against the hair and finish by brushing with it. Take your metal comb and carefully comb out and fluff up the brush on your dog's tail. Now a once-over again with the brush. Then take a small amount of liquid hair dressing and pour it on your hands a few drops at a time. Use very little. When rubbed from your hands onto the dog's coat, it will give an added sheen to the coat. Used improperly, it will make the dog look greasy. Now that you are sure of your dog's good grooming, what about your own? Don't neglect your own any more than you would your dog's. With both dog and handler "looking like a million," you're ready.

For information regarding sanctioned shows in most English-speaking areas, write to one of the kennel clubs listed below:

American Kennel Club
51 Madison Avenue
New York, NY 10010 USA

Australian Kennel Club
Royal Show Grounds
Ascot Vale, Victoria
Australia

British Kennel Club
1 Clarges Street
Piccadilly, London W1
England

Canadian Kennel Club
2150 Bloor Street West
Toronto M6S 1M8 Ontario
Canada

Irish Kennel Club
23 Earlsfort Terrace
Dublin 2
Ireland

Health and Disease

Late one night my telephone rang. It was my veterinarian. He asked if I would come over right away. He wanted to show me something that "will just break your heart." So I went over to his office and walked into the operating room where he was waiting for me.

On the operating table was a beautiful young German Shepherd. He was dead. A post-mortem was in progress. I recognized the dog at once, and to say I was shocked is a gross understatement. Only five days before I had had the big thrill of watching this dog win his first blue ribbon over a large and strong class. I had bred and raised him and followed his development with keen interest, even after I had sold him. He was such a lovable dog and so adored by his owners and their children. He had such great promise for the show ring too. And now—here he was, dead almost before his real life had begun.

What happened? He was killed by his owners, killed by them as surely as if they had fired a bullet into his brain. They decided that they should give the dog worm capsules. No, there were no worm symptoms, and they had not consulted their veterinarian to determine what kind of worms, if any, the dog did have. So they dosed the dog according to the printed directions. Seeing no worms expelled, they dosed him again—a third time—and still a fourth time. Shortly after the fourth, the dog became violently ill and collapsed. They rushed him to my veterinarian, but no one could save the dog then. He died from internal hemorrhages resulting from a ruptured bowel.

Don't Be A Dog Killer

Never administer any kind of medicine to your dog except on the direction of your veterinarian—or until after you have had years of experience!

For many years now, I have been closely associated with German Shepherds—as a student of the breed, as a breeder and exhibitor, and later as a judge. And during that time I have never seen a single indication that the German Shepherd, as a breed, is subject to or has any predisposition to a particular disease, disorder, or dysfunction. Therefore, I cannot give you a list of German Shepherd diseases. The Shepherd is, however, subject to the same illnesses that most canine flesh is heir to, and it might be well to mention some of the more common precautions and

Health and Disease

simple treatments that are required.

Prevention is the key word for many dog diseases, and the best prevention is a series of vaccinations administered by your veterinarian. Such contagious diseases as distemper, hepatitis, parainfluenza, leptospirosis, rabies, and parvovirus enteritus can be virtually eliminated by strictly following a vaccination schedule.

Distemper

This is not the place to go into a clinical discussion of distemper, its causative agents, symptoms, development, and treatment. By all means, read about it, but it needn't concern you one bit, because the first thing you must do with your puppy is to take him to your veterinarian for distemper vaccination. And your veterinarian will use any one of several systems of vaccination against distemper.

If your puppy has already had some type of distemper vaccination (or any other vaccinations) when he arrives, find out in advance from the seller what the vaccinations were and the brand names of the vaccines. This will enable your veterinarian to continue proper vaccination or to give "booster" shots. Be sure that your Shepherd puppy has this vaccination at once—and before he comes in contact with other dogs or goes where other dogs have been.

Your Dog's Medicine Cabinet

Generally speaking, your dog's medicine cabinet is not in your home. It should be at your veterinarian's! But there is one instrument you must have and must learn to use. That is a rectal thermometer, and a good one is very cheap. Buy one, and if you don't know how to use it, ask your veterinarian to show you how, and how to read it. This thermometer will save you and your veterinarian a lot of trouble, and it may well save your dog's life.

A mature dog's normal temperature is usually considered to be about 101 degrees and that of a puppy about 102 degrees. Don't hesitate to take your puppy's temperature at any time. Any time he seems listless, unusually quiet, "off his feed," or has loose bowel movements more than once or twice, check his temperature. If his temperature goes to 103, watch him carefully and check again in an hour. If it goes to 104, you have a

44

Health and Disease

really sick puppy that must be taken to the veterinarian at once. But a word of consolation here. Puppies, like human infants, are inclined to "shoot a temperature." Usually your veterinarian will be able to put it down very quickly, but anything over 103 requires his attention at once. Temperatures can come from everything from virus diseases to worms. Let your veterinarian decide what's what.

1. Flea-host tapeworm. 2. Segment of tapeworm as seen in dog's stool. 3. Common roundworm. 4. Heartworm.

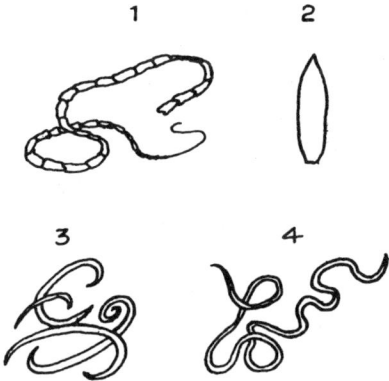

Worm Infestation

Worms are almost always present in young dogs and should be medically eliminated, the common roundworm being the most prevalent. The presence of worms and the kind of worms are to be determined by your veterinarian, after testing a stool sample from your dog. Do not administer any kind of worm medicine, except on the veterinarian's instruction. Roundworms, and less frequently, hook- and tapeworms do occur and are eliminated by different drugs. Heart worm, formerly found mostly in the south of this country or in the tropics, is now found countrywide, and its eradication in the dog is strictly the province of a highly skilled veterinarian, with diagnosis being made from a blood sample. Heart worm is something to suspect when an active, happy dog gradually slows down to the point of easy fatigue from very little activity. But I repeat, this is solely a matter for your veterinarian.

Ear mite.

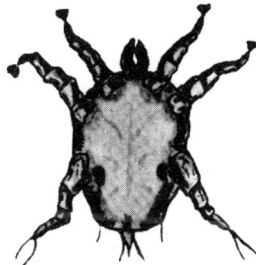

Health and Disease

The common dog flea, Ctenocephalides canis.

Fleas, Ticks, and Lice

Fleas, and in some sections, ticks occasionally occur on dogs. Their elimination has been covered in the section on grooming. Lice on the dog are rare, but stubborn to eliminate and require veterinary treatment.

Lameness

Lameness in your dog can come of any one of a number of causes, such as sprains, rheumatism, and even fractures, not to mention foreign bodies, such as nails or thorns in the feet. Have your dog examined by your veterinarian if lameness continues and you can locate no external cause.

Ear Troubles

Occasionally, a condition arises which causes the dog's ears (although usually it is one ear) to be painful to the touch. the dog tends to carry his head to one side and is apt to dig at it and cry out. A watery sound can sometimes be heard if the ear is manipulated, and frequently there is a foul odor coming from the ear. Casual examination of the inside of the ear will reveal what looks like dirt, wax, and clotted blood. This condition is commonly called "ear canker" or otitis. While it occurs rarely, its apparently quite painful to the dog; and, if treatment is not given, the inner ear may become affected, resulting in a chronic otitis or other complications. Your veterinarian may recommend one of two treatments.

Dip a cotton swab into mineral oil and carefully clean out the ear, using as many clean swabs as necessary. When the ear is well cleaned, blot up any remaining dirt or oil with a dry swab. Then, with a small bulb ear syringe containing bismuth formic iodine powder, gently dust the ear, reaching well down into the base of the ear with the powder. It is frequently necessary to repeat this treatment once or twice a day for three or four days before eliminating the irritation.

Another preparation which is effective in treating otitis is bacitracin ointment. Clean the ear well as described, then with a small gob of the ointment on the swab, work it around well into the base of the ear. Use a strong small flashlight so that you can see well into the ear to make sure your swabbing and dusting coverage is effective.

Eye Troubles

Frequently watery or discharging eyes are caused by foreign substances on the eyeball or by wind, resulting from the dog's riding with his head outside a car window (a very dangerous practice which should not be allowed). Either borated petroleum jelly or bacitracin ointment may be used. Squeeze a fair amount of either directly onto the eyeball with the lid held back slightly. then release the lid and massage the closed eye gently with a circular motion.

Repeat with the other eye. If the irritation doesn't clear up within two days, consult your veterinarian.

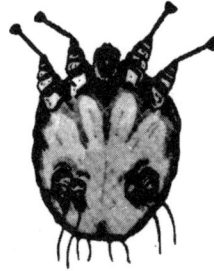

Sarcoptic mange mite.

Minor Skin Irritations

If you suspect mange or wet or dry eczema, consult your veterinarian at once. He will diagnose and direct treatment. However, countless irritations of the skin do occur, and they may be treated and eliminated by you. Any rash-like or itching spot may be dealt with by first washing the area with warm water and mild soap, then drying gently but thoroughly. After this, dust the area well with bismuth formic iodine powder. Repeat for a day or two and the irritation will usually disappear.

Health and Disease

Demodectic mange mite.

Insect bites, scratches, and very small cuts may be treated in the same manner. Do not, however, use the powder internally or around the eyes or nose.

Cuts and Wounds

Sizable cuts may be treated by first cutting the hair short around them and then washing them with mild soap and hot water. A mild dilution of an antiseptic preparation may be used to bathe the wound. Continue to bathe the wound gently every day to keep it clean. There are various antibiotic ointments available that may promote healing. However, such preparations will usually be licked off by the patient

and hence are apt to be of little value.

If the cut is large enough to require bandaging, you should have your veterinarian deal with it. Dogs are incredibly handy and quick at removing such dressings, and it is occasionally necessary to use a loose muzzle or Elizabethan collar of aluminum or heavy cardboard to prevent removal of dressings. Gaping wounds should be treated by your veterinarian as fast as it is possible to get your dog to him. Unless sutured almost at once, the two torn edges of the wound will not heal properly. Speed in treatment is vital. This also applies to ripped ears from fights or barbed wire.

Incessant and heavy bleeding must be stopped by your veterinarian, and, again, speed is of the essence. As a first-aid measure while taking the dog to the veterinarian, try to locate a "pressure point" and, with a wad of gauze or clean cloth, press to stem the flow of blood.

Always remember that a painfully injured or badly frightened dog is apt to bite at anything—including you. Before attempting to handle a dog in a state of shock, the mouth must be bandaged or tied shut. A man's necktie is good in an emergency. Wrap the material

Health and Disease

around the dog's muzzle (foreface) by first laying it over the top of the muzzle, then crossing it under the lower jaw, then bringing it up around the back of the neck, just behind and below the ear base. There, tie your improvised bandage in a firm knot and proceed. Be sure that the mouth bandage is loose enough so that the dog can open his mouth to pant, but not enough to bite. Repeat: Dogs of all breeds are quite apt to bite if they are painfully injured. It's a strictly impersonal action. The dog has no idea that it may be your fingers he has hold of. And in regard to first-aid treatment and handling, especially bandaging, your veterinarian will give you the necessary instruction.

Puncture wounds, such as those from nails or those sustained during a fight, are usually deep and difficult to deal with. They require immediate treatment, and your veterinarian is the person to do it, as soon as possible after the injury.

Car Sickness

Most young dogs have to learn to ride in a car, and in so doing, they frequently become nauseated and vomit. Usually, this is due to the excitement of the new method of travel rather than to the motions of the car. First, let your puppy sit in a parked car until he feels at home in it. Do this over a period of several days. Then, take him on very short trips—say a mile or two or three. If he is restless and begins to drool heavily, stop the car, put on his leash, and take him for a walk or a romp for a few minutes. Then back into the car and home again. Avoid car trips just before and just after feeding.

If, however, your dog fails to outgrow car sickness after a few weeks, your veterinarian will give you a sedative to give the dog before trips.

Vomiting

There is perhaps no animal that can vomit with the speed and ease of a dog. Usually, the event means nothing. A puppy will sometimes vomit a feeding if fed too soon after violent exercise—or from just plain eating too fast—and most dogs eat very rapidly. Dogs will also eat green grass and shortly after toss up the grass. Some bitches with a litter develop an annoying habit of eating their own feeding, jumping in with the puppies, and promptly throwing up the entire feeding for the puppies

Health and Disease

to eat—which they do with great relish, and it is not in any way harmful. Another cause of vomiting is the strong hydrochloric acid content of the digestive juices of certain individual dogs. I had a dog that would vomit up this digestive juice if he was not fed right "on the button" of the usual time. All of these causes and results are merely annoying to you. Persistent vomiting or regular daily vomiting or the vomiting of blood should prompt you to see your veterinarian without delay.

Diarrhea And Loose Bowels

Intestinal disorders may be caused by such a wide variety of things that I cannot recommend that you attempt treatment at home. There are many simple treatments with widely available preparations which will quickly correct the situation, but play it safe—talk with your veterinarian, meanwhile withholding liquids and food until you have advice from him. The presence of blood in a loose bowel movement is cause for alarm, and you should have the dog examined at once.

Constipation

Rarely, if ever, will a properly fed puppy become constipated, but in the event that he does become constipated, give him two teaspoonfuls of milk of magnesia—one teaspoonful in a very young puppy.

Rabies

Let no one doubt that there does exist a terrifying disease called rabies. It is brought about by infecting the blood stream of any warm-blooded animal with the causative virus from a diseased animal. Naturally, the disease is transmitted by a diseased animal's biting a healthy one, the virus entering the blood stream or traveling along the nerve roots of the healthy animal through the puncture wounds of the teeth. I have gone to considerable trouble and mileage to observe two cases—both forms, the so-called "dumb rabies" in which the jaw is paralyzed, and the "wild rabies" in which instance the victim hurries around, snapping at and biting both living and inanimate things. I repeat, it is a hideous disease. It is a public health menace, not to mention the fact that it is a violent and acutely painful sure-death for its victims.

As I have said, with some difficulty I have observed but two cases of rabies in my lifetime. There

Health and Disease

are many veterinarians who have practiced for years who have never seen a single case, aside from what may have been induced artificially for research purposes. It is my considered and firm opinion that real and terrible as the disease is, it is a rare disease in dogs.

A great deal of time and money has been spent in trying to develop a vaccine effective against this horrible disease. Have your dog vaccinated against rabies.

How To Give Medicines

Liquids: Do not open the mouth. Instead, pull out the lower lip at the corner of the mouth and pour the medicine in with a spoon or bottle. If the dog holds the medicine in his mouth, he can be made to swallow it by opening the mouth slightly.

Hold the head only very slightly upward. (If the head is held too high, the medicine may enter the windpipe instead of the passage to the stomach, thus choking the dog.) For vicious animals, the medicine can still be given by this method, even though the dog's mouth is held shut with a tape or a muzzle.

Pills or tablets: Open the dog's mouth by placing your left thumb on the roof of the mouth behind the canine tooth. Pressure with the thumb will make nearly all dogs open their mouths, and they seem unable to close them until the pressure is released. With the right hand, place the pill or tablet far back on the tongue, then take out your thumb and close the mouth. The dog will swallow the medicine.

Powders are given similarly, except that powders are *dropped* on the back of the tongue.

For further medical or health information, refer to *The Dog Owner's Encyclopedia of Veterinary Medicine* (published by T.F.H. Publications and available wherever the book you are now reading was purchased). This immensely useful and practical guide to the recognition and treatment of a dog's medical and surgical problems should be on every dog owner's bookshelf.

Breeding and Whelping

So you have a female German Shepherd and you want to breed her for a litter of puppies. Wonderful idea—very simple—lot of fun—make a lot of money. Well, it *is* a wonderful idea, but stop right there. It's not very simple—and you won't make a lot of money. Having a litter of puppies to bring up is hard, painstaking, thoughtful work. If this doesn't bother you, then it can be fun.

Breed Better Dogs

Bear in mind this very important point: Being a breeder of German Shepherds is not just breeding dear Tillie to that darned good-looking

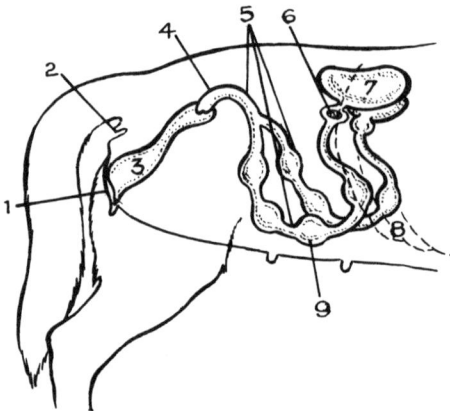

Reproductive system of the male German Shepherd. 1. Penis. 1a. Sheath. 2. Testicle. 3. Scrotum. 4. Pelvic bone. 5. Anus. 6. Rectum. 7. Prostate. 8. Bladder. 9. Vas deferens.

Reproductive system of the female German Shepherd. 1. Vulva. 2. Anus. 3. Vagina. 4. Cervix. 5. Uterus. 6. Ovary. 7. Kidneys. 8. Ribs. 9. Fetal lump.

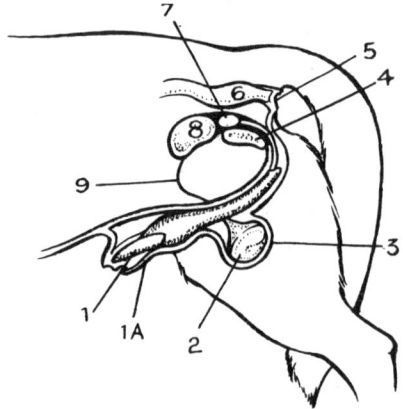

male Shepherd down the street. Would that it were that simple! Such a breeding will undoubtedly produce puppies. But that is not all you want. When you breed your female, it is only after the most careful planning, with every effort being made to be sure that the resulting puppies will be even better than the parent dogs—that they will come even closer to the standard than the parent animals—and that all the puppies will have good homes. Any fool can breed a litter of puppies, but only a careful, thoughtful, intelligent person can breed a litter of better German Shepherd puppies. That must be your goal in breeding!

You can become a good novice breeder if you truly love German

Breeding and Whelping

Shepherds and are seriously concerned with the past, present, and future of the magnificent breed. You will breed your female only according to established scientific principles. Your personal sentiments have no place in this project whatever and must have no place in the careful planning that goes on before you actually breed your female. The science of mammalian genetics is not a precise science like, say, mathematics. And the extensive reading you will do on the science (or art) of breeding dogs before you start to choose a stud will give you some idea of the variable factors you will be dealing with. It is a vast subject, but with a few brief pointers here and additional reading and study, you can at least start on the right track.

Plan It On Paper

The principles of animal breeding are the same, whether the subjects be beef cattle, poultry, or dogs. To quote a cattleman friend of mine, every breeding is first made "on paper" and later in the barnyard. In other words, first the blood strains of the animals are considered as to what goes well with what, so far as recorded ancestry is concerned.

Having worked this out, the two animals to be mated must be studied and compared. If one does not excel where the other is lacking, at least in most points, then the paper planning must start over again and different animals are considered.

With your own Shepherd, there are several "musts" that are really axioms. First, breed only the best to the best. Two inferior animals will produce nothing but inferior animals, as surely as night follows day. To breed an inferior Shepherd to another inferior one is a crime against the breed. So start by breeding the best to the best. And here again, an accurate knowledge of the Shepherd standard is essential to know just what is best.

"Compensation" Breeding

No perfect dog has yet been whelped. Your Shepherd female may be a winning show dog. She may be a champion. But she does have faults. In breeding her to a fine male, we must consider "compensation" breeding. She must compensate for his shortcomings and he for hers. For example, your female may be ideal in most respects but have thin, spread, faulty feet. So the male you choose, which is ideal in other

Breeding and Whelping

respects, *must* have ideal feet, as had his sire and dam too. In this way you may overcome the foot faults in yor female's puppies.

This same principle applies to the correction of faults in any section of either male or female. But, you say, my dog has a pedigree as long as your arm. Must be good! Sad but true, a pedigree will not necessarily produce good puppies. A pedigree is no more—and no less—than your dog's recorded ancestry. Yes, you must know what dogs are in your dog's pedigree, but the most important point is were they good dogs? What were their faults and virtues? And to what degree did these dogs transmit these faults and virtues?

Line-Breeding

Now you may have heard that "like begets like." This is true and it is also false! Likes can beget likes only when both parent animals have the same likeness through generations of both family lines. The only way known to "fix" virtues and to eliminate faults is to mate two dogs of fairly close relationship bloodwise, two dogs which come from generations of likes and are family related in their likeness. In this way you may

ensure a higher and regular percentage of puppies which can be expected to mature into adults at least free from major faults under the standard. The likes must have the same genetic inheritance.

Through this "family" breeding all correct type is set and maintained. If both family lines are sound to begin with, family breeding and even close inbreeding will merely improve the strain—but only in skilled hands. The finest German Shepherds today are the result of just such breeding methods. Study, expert advice, and experience will enable you, a novice, to follow these principles. So in your planning, forget the old nonsense about idiots and two-headed monsters coming from related parents.

Then too, in your planning and reading, remember that intangible virtues, as well as physical ones, are without doubt inherited, as are faults in those intangibles. For example, in breeding bird dogs where "nose sense" is of greatest importance, this factor can to a degree be fixed for future generations of puppies, when the ancestors on both sides have the virtue of "nose sense." Just so other characteristics of disposition or temperament can be fixed.

Care of Mother and Family

Let us assume that you have selected the right stud dog for your female and that she has been bred. In some 58 to 60 days, you will be presented with a nice litter of German Shepherd puppies. But there are a number of things to be gone over and prepared in advance of the whelping date.

Before your female was bred, she was, of course, checked by your veterinarian and found to be in good condition and free from worms of any sort. She was in good weight but not fat.

There's an old saying, "a litter should be fed from the day the bitch is bred," and there is a world of truth in it. So from the day your female is bred right up to the time the puppies are fully weaned, the mother's food is of the greatest importance. Puppies develop very rapidly in their 58 to 60 days of gestation, and their demands on the mother's system for nourishment are great. In effect, you are feeding your female and perhaps seven or eight other dogs, all at the same time.

Additions To Regular Diet

For the first 21 days, your female will need but few additions to her regular diet. Feed her as usual, except for the addition of about a quarter-pound of "pot" or cottage cheese. This cheese, made from sour milk, is an ideal, natural source of added protein, calcium, and phosphorus—all essential to the proper growth of the unborn litter. It is my conviction, after a good deal of experimentation, that commercial vitamin-mineral supplements are unnecessary if the mother is fed the proper selection of natural foods.

Most commercial supplements are absolutely loaded with mineral calcium. You will usually find that the bulk of the contents is just plain calcium, a cheap and plentiful substance. Necessary as it is, there is no doubt whatever in my mind that calcium from an animal source like cheese is far more readily assimilated and is much cheaper besides. At any rate, if you choose to follow what I suggest for feeding, do not use a commercial supplement without consulting your veterinarian and telling him the diet your dog is already getting.

Increase Food Intake

Along about the fifth week, the litter will begin to show a little, and now is the time to start an increase in food intake, not so much in bulk

Care of Mother and Family

as in nutritive strength. Increase the cottage cheese intake to half a pound per day, gradually increasing to a full pound per day. From this cheese, your female is getting the necessary food value, without the bulk, of quarts of liquid milk.

Her appetite has notably increased by now, so increase her basic meal ration with the regular amount of added fat included. To this regular ration, add one-half pound of slightly cooked pork liver (because pork liver is the cheapest). Cut this into small pieces or grind it and mix with the basic ration. Alternate beef or veal heart, fed raw but finely cut up. Liver, however, perhaps more than any other one thing, will help produce in your female a heavy supply of milk with which to nurse the coming puppies. Milk does not produce milk! Liver, in addition to all its other high nutritive qualities, helps to produce milk. Continue feeding slightly cooked liver until the puppies are five to six weeks old, then decrease.

Feed Several Times A Day

By now, your female is but a few weeks away from her whelping date, and the growing puppies are compressing her internal organs to an uncomfortable degree. She will have to relieve herself with greater frequency now. The stomach, too, is being compressed, so try reducing the basic ration slightly and at the same time increase the meats and cottage cheese. Feed several small meals per day in order to get in the proper, stepped-up quantity of food without causing the increased pressure of a single large meal.

Regular Exercise Important

A great deal of advice has been given by experts on keeping the female quiet from the day she is

German Shepherds are strong and active dogs. It will be unkind to confine them in a small area. These dogs need ample space to keep well. p. 57, above; It is advantageous to choose your German Shepherd puppy from a litter, preferably with both or at least one of the parents. p. 57, below; Retrieving exercises can be fun for both your German Shepherd and you. p. 58; What a lovely picture of domestic bliss. A German Shepherd dam is just as protective of her young as she is of her human "family." p. 59; (Left to right) In action at the long jump in Obedience trial. Six well-behaved adult representatives of the breed. Being judged at a conformation show. p. 60-61, upper row; (Left) Anticipating the arrival of the master of the house. (Right) Out in the open enjoying the great outdoors. p. 60-61, lower row; These faces show an alert disposition and keen intelligence. p. 62-63; German Shepherds have made their mark as both show and working dogs. p. 64.

60

WINNERS

NATIONAL CAPITAL
KENNEL CLUB, INC.

64

Care of Mother and Family

bred all through the pregnancy. I say to you that such quiet is not natural and it cannot be enforced. Naturally, the female should not be permitted to go in for fence jumping, but she will be as active as ever during the first few weeks and gradually she will, of her own accord, slow down appropriately, since no one knows quite as much about having puppies as the dog herself—up to a point. But see to it that your female has plenty of gentle exercise all the way along. She'll let you know when she wants to slow down. Treat her normally, and don't let her be the victim of all the sentimentality that humans with impending families are heir to.

Whelping Imminent

About the morning of the 58th day or shortly thereafter, your female, who now looks like an outsize beer barrel, will suddenly refuse her food. She may drink water, however. If you have been observant as things progressed, your hand, if not your eye, will tell you that the litter has dropped. The female now has a saggy abdomen, and this is the tip-off that whelping will occur soon, usually well within the next 24 hours. As the actual

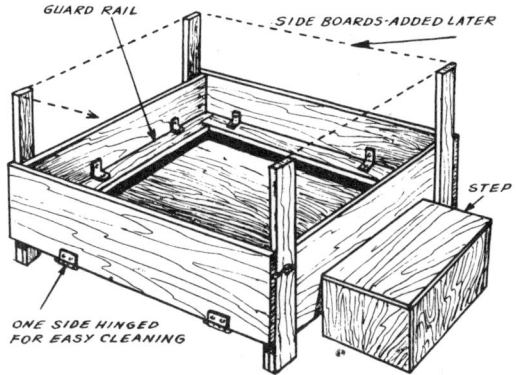

Whelping box.

whelping hour approaches, the mother will become increasingly restless. She will seek out dark places like closets. She will scratch at the floor and wad up rugs as if making a bed. She is pretty miserable right now, so be gently sympathetic with her but *not* maudlin!

Get her to stay in the whelping box you have had prepared for several days. This box should be in a fairly quiet place and consist of an area of about four feet by six feet fenced off with an edging of boards about six inches high. There should be a solid, heavy linoleum floor. This makes for easy wiping up, and the mother will be less apt to scratch it up or tear it. You may lay newspapers over the linoleum for absorbency, although she'll probably

65

Care of Mother and Family

have them all scratched into a pile before she even gets started.

Warmth Essential

The whelping area should be located in a warm, not hot, place free from drafts. You may, if you wish, confine her to the box by hitching her there with a leash, fastening the upper end of the leash to a hook three or four feet off the floor so she won't get twisted up in it. But when actual whelping starts, take off both leash and collar. Then, get yourself a chair and prepare for an all-night vigil. Somehow puppies always seem to be born at night, and the process is good for 12 to 14 hours usually.

There is great difference of opinion as to whether to stay with her or leave her alone when she starts to whelp. My advice is to stay right with her, you and possibly one other person she knows well. No audience please! A supply of warm water, old turkish towels, and plenty of wiping rags is in order at this point.

When labor commences, the female usually assumes a squatting position, although some prefer to lie down. The first puppy won't look much like a puppy to you when it is fully expelled from the female. It will be wrapped in a dark,

membranous sac, which the mother will tear open with her teeth exposing one small, noisy Shepherd— very wet. Let the mother lick the puppy off and help to dry it. She will also bite off the navel cord. This may make the puppy squeal but don't worry, mama is not trying to eat her child. When she is through cleaning the puppy off, pick up the puppy and gently but firmly give it a good rubbing with a turkish towel. Do this in full sight of the mother and close enough so that she will not leave her whelping box.

Keep Puppies Separate

When the puppy is good and dry and "squawking" a bit, place it in a shallow paper box close to the mother so she can see it but will not step on it when she becomes restless with labor for the second puppy. If the room temperature is lower than 70 degrees, place a hot water bottle wrapped in a towel in the box under the puppies. Be sure to keep the water changed and warm so the puppies aren't lying on a cold water bottle. Constant warmth is essential.

After each puppy has arrived and been cleaned up, add it to those in the paper box. If, however, there is

Care of Mother and Family

a long wait between puppies, place those already born close to the mother so that they will start to suckle. For some reason, this action seems to stimulate labor. Put the puppies back in the box when labor begins again.

German Shepherds, as a breed, are easy whelpers, so you need not anticipate any trouble. Just stay with

Trough for holding nursing bottles.

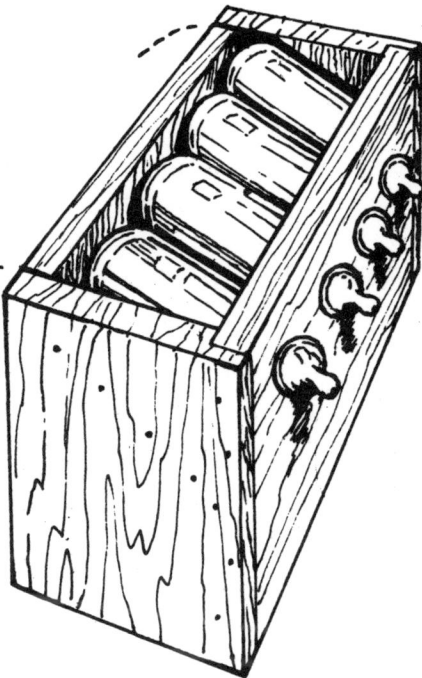

the mother more as an observer than anything else. Remember dogs have been having puppies for years now!

Post-Natal Care

When you are reasonably certain that the mother has finished whelping, have your veterinarian administer the proper amount of obstetrical pituitrin. This drug will induce labor again, thus helping to expel any retained afterbirth or dead puppy.

Inspect your puppies carefully. Rarely will any deformities be found, but if there should be any, make a firm decision to have your veterinarian destroy the puppy or puppies showing deformities.

Check the hind legs of each puppy carefully for dewclaws. These occur occasionally and should be removed by your veterinarian. If not removed, they are not only disfiguring, but located as they are, they are constantly subject to injury. So it's better all around to have them removed.

During and after whelping, the female is very much dehydrated, so at frequent intervals she should be offered lukewarm milk or meat soup, slightly thickened with well-soaked regular ration. She will relish liquids and soft foods for about 24 hours, after which she will go back to her regular diet. But

Care of Mother and Family

be sure she has a constant supply of fresh water available. Feed her and keep her water container outside the whelping box.

The puppies will be blind for about 15 days, with the eyes gradually opening up at that time. The little Shepherds will be quite active and crawl about over a large area. You have little to do with the puppies now until they are about three weeks of age, at which time I believe they should be started on supplementary feeding.

Weaning Time

Feeding puppies is a highly controversial subject. I have tried nearly every known system. Recently, I raised two litters of puppies exclusively on a

Good specimen of male puppy at three months of age.

pellet dog food, with no supplements of any sort added except melted animal fat; no milk, no meat, no anything else. These puppies are now over a year old. All are well-grown, heavy-boned, deep-bodied animals that I am proud to have

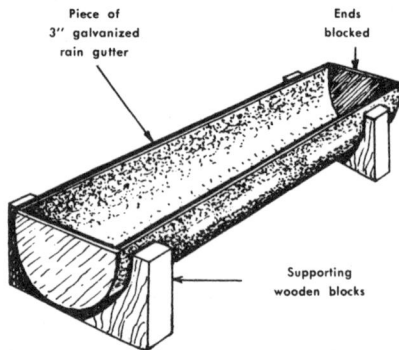

Water trough for puppies; a trough like this also can be used for holding food.

my name on. They are scattered over a wide area, but I have made it a point to keep a check on each one. Several are already winning in the show ring.

While I personally shall continue to feed puppies in this manner, the choice is yours or your veterinarian's. I have seen various breeds of dogs fed in this manner in research kennels and all are in top shape, breeding normally and producing fine puppies. These puppies in turn, being fed the same way, have matured and raised third, fourth, and fifth generations—all on this method of feeding. To me, then, it is a good way to feed.

To Spay Or Not To Spay

To spay a female dog (past tense, spayed) is to remove both ovaries from the dog surgically, thus rendering it impossible for the dog ever to have puppies or periods of "heat" or "season." And make no mistake about it, this is major surgery to be performed only by a graduate, licensed veterinarian. However, in his hands, the practice of spaying is quite generally used and is considered a routine operation. The risk involved is almost zero, assuming that the dog is of correct age and is in excellent health and condition.

Needless to say, there is considerable difference of opinion on spaying. "Spay and spoil your female" is the contention of those who are opposed, although just how the female is "spoiled" I have never been able to discover. The opponents will tell you that the spayed female becomes sluggish, dull, has no pep or joy in life, gets enormously fat, and wants only to eat and sleep. It is further alleged that the spayed female is rendered stupid and unable to learn anything.

Improves Companionship

Now, among old-timers in the dog game, there is a very strong conviction that the female is a far better companion and housedog than the male, and the best housedog and companion is a spayed female. I have owned two myself and I certainly agree that the spayed female is indeed the almost perfect companion. I have never seen a fat, stupid spayed female. In my experience and observation, spaying in no way affects the personality or characteristic joy in living of the German Shepherd. Granted, there is a tendency to get fat. But this situation is easily regulated by proper feeding.

To anyone not interested in breeding dogs but who wants a fine companion and housedog, the spayed German Shepherd female has no superior. Always beautiful anyway, she is keen, smart, and lively. As for spaying making a dog stupid, the whole argument goes out the window with the mention of one fact. The Seeing Eye, Inc., regularly spays all its females trained as guide dogs for the blind.

Caring For The Brood Bitch

If your female German Shepherd is to be used as a breeding animal, there are certain topics to be covered in the management of the

69

To Spay or Not to Spay

female during her periods of heat.

The female Shepherd usually comes in heat for the first time between the ages of seven and 12 months, usually around ten months in my own experience. And allowing for some variations in individual dogs, the female will come in heat roughly twice a year, once in the spring and once in the fall or thereabouts.

The onset of the heat period is marked by a slight discharge of dark red blood from the vulva or external genital organ of the female. With this discharge, odorless to humans, comes a gradual swelling and enlargement of the vulva, along with an increased flow of blood, until the ninth or tenth day, at which time the vulva is quite enlarged and the flow has begun to be pinkish or amber colored. The discharge gradually pales out and decreases during the third week. But while the heat period is usually considered to be three weeks, it is much safer to count it a month in duration.

Preventing Accidental Breeding

If you live in the city, the heat period will cause you little if any inconvenience, since, in the city,

dogs are more apt to be leashed or more carefully controlled than dogs in the suburbs and country. But the safe rule, to guard against accidental breeding, is to keep your female always on a lead throughout the entire heat period. As for the droplets of discharge around the house, they are odorless and may easily be removed by wiping with a damp cloth.

In the country or suburbs, you may have somewhat of a problem. Again, take your female outside only on a leash and keep her close beside you. If possible, walk her a little way from the house to relieve herself, keeping a sharp lookout for visiting males. Some males are extremely fast operators, and unless you are very careful, especially from the seventh or eighth day on, you may have an unwanted breeding before you know it. In this instance, once such a breeding has begun, there is absolutely nothing you can do about it. Attempted separation of the two animals will result in serious injury to both. However, should you have such bad luck, immediately take your female to your veterinarian. Sometimes he can prevent a litter of mutts.

Indoors, continue your caution. Along about the eleventh or twelfth day, your female may sneak outside

Care of the Oldster

if not watched, and she is sure to run into a group of waiting males. Keep her under lock and key for a full month!

There are various preparations on the market which allegedly discourage male dogs from hanging around. They are usually liquids with a strong, pungent odor designed to fool the nose of the males. In my experience, none of these preparations is reliable.

Choose a healthy pup and you'll be assured of enjoying your German Shepherd for many years as he passes into handsome adulthood and then into his "golden years" of old age.

As a breed, German Shepherds are not inclined, as some breeds are, to early aging. Barring accident or disease, they are apt to enjoy a life of 12 to 14 years. However, beginning roughly with the eighth year, there will be gradual slowing down. And with this there are many problems of maintaining reasonably good health and comfort for all concerned.

While there is little or nothing that can be done in the instance of failing sight and hearing, proper management of the dog can minimize these losses. Fairly close and carefully supervised confinement are necessary in both cases. A blind dog, otherwise perfectly healthy and happy, can continue to be happy if he is always on a leash outdoors and guided so that he does not bump into things. Indoors, he will do well enough on his own. Dogs that are sightless seem to move around the house by their own radar system. They learn where objects are located, such as chairs, tables, doors, and so on. Once they do learn the pattern, care must be taken not to leave a piece of furniture out of its usual place. But I am flatly opposed to sending any dog to the Great Beyond because it is blind or deaf—if it is otherwise healthy and seems to enjoy life.

Care of the Oldster

Deafness again requires considerable confinement, especially in regard to motor traffic and similar hazards, but deafness curtails the dog's activities much less than blindness.

Teeth in the aging dog should be watched carefully, not only for the pain they may cause the dog but especially because they may poison the system without any local infection or pain. So watch carefully, especially when an old dog is eating. Any departure from his usual manner should make teeth suspect at once. Have your veterinarian check the teeth frequently. If necessary, they may all be removed, and the dog will continue in good health and comfort.

As His System Slows Down

As the dog ages and slows down in his physical activity, so his whole system slows down. With the change, physical functions are in some instances slowed and in others accelerated—in effect, at least.

For example, constipation may occur, and bowel movements may become difficult, infrequent, or even painful. Chronic constipation is a problem for your veterinarian to deal with, but unless it is chronic, it is easily dealt with by adding a little extra melted fat to the regular food. Do not increase roughage or administer physics unless so directed by your veterinarian. If the added fat in the food doesn't seem to be the answer to occasional constipation, give your dog a half or full teaspoon of mineral oil two or three times a week. Otherwise, call your veterinarian.

On either side of the rectal opening, just below the base of thetail, are located the two anal glands. Occasionally these glands do not function properly and may cause the dog great discomfort if not cleaned out. This is a job for your veterinarian, until after he has shown you how to do it. It is a comparatively simple job once you learn how, although it isn't the most pleasant in the world.

Watch His Weight

In feeding the aging dog, try to keep his weight down. He may want just as much to eat as ever, but with decreased activity, he will tend to put on weight. This weight will tend to slow down all other bodily functions and place an added strain on the heart. So feed the same diet

Care of the Oldster

as usual, but watch the weight.

Age, with its relaxing of the muscles, frequently makes an otherwise clean dog begin to misbehave in the house, particularly so far as urination is concerned. There is little that can be done about it, after your veterinarian finds there is no infection present, except to give your dog more frequent chances to urinate and move his bowels. It's just a little bit more work on your part to keep your old friend more comfortable and a "good" dog.

Let your dog exercise as much as he wants to without encouraging him in any violent play. If he is especially sluggish, take him for a mile walk on a leash in the early morning or late evening. Avoid exercise for him during the heat of the day. And in cold weather or rain, try a blanket on him when he goes out. It's not "sissy" to put a coat on an old Shepherd. Even Army dogs wore them under some conditions. You and your veterinarian, working closely together, can give your dog added life and comfort. So consult your veterinarian often.

Occasionally in an old dog, there is a problem of unpleasant smell, both bodily and orally. If this situation is acute, it is an all but unbearable to have the dog around. But the situation can be corrected or at least alleviated with a frequent and rather heavy dosing of chlorophyll. And a teaspoon of milk of magnesia three or four times a week may also prove beneficial. A good rubdown with one of the dry shampoo products is also helpful.

When The End Comes

People who have dogs are sooner or later faced with the tragedy of losing them. It's tough business losing a dog, no matter how many you may have at one time. And one dog never takes the place of another—so don't expect it to. When you lose your dog, get another as quickly as you can. It does help a lot. And you have the joy of always having a wonderful German Shepherd with you, even though it's a different one.

Keep your dog alive as long as he is happy and comfortable. Do everything you reasonably can to keep him that way. But when the sad time comes that he is sick, always uncomfortable, or in some pain, it is your obligation then to have him put away. It is a tough ordeal to go through, but you owe it to your old friend to allow him to

Official Breed Standard

go to sleep. And literally that's just what he does. Your veterinarian knows what to do. And your good old Shepherd, without pain, fright, bad taste, or bad smells, will just drift off to sleep. Most Shepherd owners, because they loved their old dog, will pay him the greatest possible tribute. He proved that there's nothing quite so wonderful as a fine German Shepherd, so in his honor they'll get another German Shepherd as soon as they can. I think he'd like it that way.

The physical appearance of your German Shepherd pup has been predetermined by genetic inheritance, but good care and nutrition will ensure that he assumes the noble profile of the breed when he matures.

GENERAL APPEARANCE: The first impression of a good German Shepherd Dog is that of a strong, agile, well-muscled animal, alert and full of life. It is well balanced, with harmonious development of the forequarter and hindquarter. The dog is longer than tall, deep-bodied, and presents an outline of smooth curves rather than angles. It looks substantial and not spindly, giving the impression, both at rest and in motion, of muscular fitness and nimbleness without any look of clumsiness or soft living. The ideal dog is stamped with a look of quality and nobility—difficult to define, but unmistakable when present. Secondary sex characteristics are strongly marked, and every animal gives a definite impression of masculinity or femininity, according to its sex.

CHARACTER: The breed has a distinct personality marked by direct and fearless, but not hostile, expression, self-confidence and a certain aloofness that does not lend itself to immediate and indiscriminate friendships. The dog must be approachable, quietly standing its ground and showing confidence and willingness to meet overtures without itself making them. It is poised, but when the occasion demands, eager and alert; both fit and willing to serve

Official Breed Standard

in its capacity as companion, watchdog, blind leader, herding dog, or guardian, whichever the circumstances may demand. The dog must not be timid, shrinking behind its master or handler; it should not be nervous, looking about or upward with anxious expression or showing nervous reactions, such as tucking of tail, to strange sounds or sights. Lack

Faulty bitch: sway back; false front assembly; overly long in body and loin; legs too short and pasterns weak; neck too short; tail curled and set too high.

of confidence under any surroundings is not typical of good character. Any of the above deficiencies in character which indicate shyness must be penalized as very serious faults and any dog exhibiting pronounced indications of these must be excused from the ring. It must be possible for the judge to observe the teeth and to determine that both testicles are descended. Any dog that attempts to bite the judge must be disqualified.

The ideal dog is a working animal with an incorruptible character combined with body and gait suitable for the arduous work that constitutes its primary purpose.

HEAD: The head is noble, cleanly chiseled, strong without coarseness, but above all not fine, and in proportion to the body. The head of the male is distinctly masculine, and that of the bitch distinctly feminine. The muzzle is long and strong with the lips firmly fitted, and its topline is paralled to the topline of the skull. Seen from the front, the forehead is only moderately arched and the skull slopes into the long, wedge-shaped muzzle without abrupt stop. Jaws are strongly developed. *Ears:* Ears are moderately pointed, in proportion to the skull, open toward the front, and carried erect when at attention, the ideal carriage being one in which the center lines of the ears, viewed from the front, are paralled to each other and perpendicular to the ground. A dog with cropped or hanging ears must be disqualified. *Eyes:* Of medium size, almond shaped, set a little obliquely and not protruding. The color is as dark as possible. The expression keen, intelligent and composed. *Teeth:* 42 in number—20 upper and 22 lower—are strongly

Official Breed Standard

developed and meet in a scissors bite in which part of the inner surface of the upper incisors meet and engage part of the outer suface of the lower incisors. An overshot jaw or a level bite is undesirable. An undershot jaw is a disqualifying fault. Complete dentition is to be preferred. Any missing teeth other than first premolars is a serious fault.

Typical male German Shepherd head.

NECK: The neck is strong and muscular, clean-cut and relatively long, proportionate in size to the head and without loose folds of skin. When the dog is at attention or excited, the head is raised and the neck carried high; otherwise typical carriage of the head is forward rather than up and but little higher than the top of the shoulders, particularly in motion.

FOREQUARTERS: The shoulder blades are long and obliquely angled, laid on flat and not placed forward. The upper arm joins the shoulder blade at about a right angle. Both the upper arm and the shoulder blade are well muscled. The forelegs, viewed from all sides, are straight and the bone oval rather than round. The pasterns are strong and springy and angulated at approximately a 25-degree angle from the vertical.

FEET: The feet are short, compact, with toes well arched, pads thick and firm, nails short and dark. The dewclaws, if any, should be removed from the hind legs. Dewclaws on the forelegs may be removed, but are normally left on.

PROPORTION: The German Shepherd Dog is longer than tall, with the most desirable proportion as 10 to 8½. The desired height for males at the top of the highest point of the shoulder blade is 24 to 26 inches; and for bitches, 22 to 24 inches. The length is measured from the point of the prosternum or breastbone to the rear edge of the pelvis, the ischial tuberosity.

BODY: The whole structure of

the body gives an impression of depth and solidity without bulkiness. *Chest:* Commencing at the prosternum, it is well filled and carried well down between the legs. It is deep and capacious, never shallow, with ample room for lungs and heart, carried well forward, with the prosternum showing ahead of the shoulder in profile.

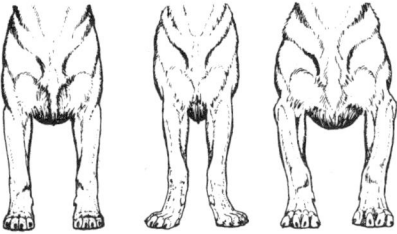

Left to right: *Excellent front; Faulty front (east and west, pinched elbows, too narrow); Faulty front (barrel-legged, loaded shoulders, poor feet).*

Ribs: Well sprung and long, neither barrel-shaped nor too flat, and carried down to a sternum which reaches to the elbows. Correct ribbing allows the elbows to move back freely when the dog is at a trot. Too round causes interference and throws the elbows out; too flat or short causes pinched elbows. Ribbing is carried well back so that the loin is relatively short. *Abdomen:* Firmly held and not paunchy. The bottom line is only moderately tucked up in the loin.

TOPLINE: *Withers:* The withers are higher than and sloping into the level back. *Back:* The back is straight, very strongly developed without sag or roach, and relatively short. The desirable long proportion is not derived from a long back, but from over-all length with relation to height, which is achieved by length of forequarter and length of withers and hindquarter, viewed from the side. *Loin:* Viewed from the top, broad and strong. Undue length between the last rib and the thigh, when viewed from the side, is undesirable. *Croup:* Long and gradually sloping.

TAIL: Bushy, with the last vertebra extended at least to the hock joint. It is set smoothly into the croup and low rather than high. At rest, the tail hangs in a slight curve like a saber. A slight hook—sometimes carried to one side—is faulty only to the extent that it mars general appearance. When the dog is excited or in motion, the curve is accentuated and the tail raised, but it should never be curled forward beyond a vertical line. Tails too short, or with clumpy ends due to ankylosis, are serious faults. A dog with a docked tail must be disqualified.

HINDQUARTERS: The whole assembly of the thigh, viewed from

the side, is broad, with both upper and lower thigh well muscled, forming as nearly as possible a right angle. The upper thigh bone parallels the shoulder blade while the lower thigh bone parallels the upper arm. The metatarsus (the unit between the hock joint and the foot) is short, strong and tightly articulated.

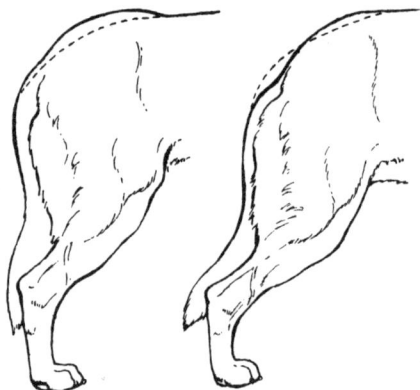

Overbuilt; high hock. Steep, short croup.

GAIT: A German Shepherd Dog is a trotting dog, and its structure has been developed to meet the requirements of its work. *General Impression:* The gait is outreaching, elastic, seemingly without effort, smooth and rhythmic covering the maximum amount of ground with the minimum number of steps. At a walk it covers a great deal of ground, with long stride of both hind legs and forelegs. At a trot the dog covers still more ground with even longer stride, and moves powerfully but easily, with co-ordination and balance so that the gait appears to be the steady motion of a well-lubricated machine. The feet travel close to the ground on both forward reach and backward push. In order to achieve ideal movement of this kind, there must be good muscular development and ligamentation. The hindquarters deliver, through the back, a powerful forward thrust which slightly lifts the whole animal and drives the body forward. Reaching far under, and passing the imprint left by the front foot, the hind foot takes hold of the ground; then hock, stifle and upper thigh come into play and sweep back, the stroke of the hind leg finishing with the foot still close to the ground in a smooth follow-through. The over-reach of the hindquarter usually necessitates one hind foot passing outside and the other hind foot passing inside the track of the forefeet, and such action is not faulty unless the locomotion is crabwise with the dog's body sideways out of the normal straight line.

TRANSMISSION: The typical smooth, flowing gait is maintained with great strength and firmness of back. The whole effort of the hindquarter is transmitted to the forequarter through the loin, back and withers. At full trot, the back must remain firm and level without sway, roll, whip or roach. Unlevel topline with withers lower than the hip is a fault. To compensate for the forward motion imparted by the hindquarters, the shoulder should open to its full extent. The forelegs should reach out close to the ground in a long stride in harmony with that of the hindquarters. The dog does not track on widely separated paralled lines, but brings the feet inward toward the middle line of the body when trotting in order to maintain balance. The feet rack closely but do not strike or cross over. Viewed from the front, the front legs function from the shoulder joint to the pad in a staight line. Viewed from the rear, the hind legs function from the hip joint to the pad in a straight line. Faults of gait, whether from front, rear or side, are to be considered very serious faults.

COLOR: The German Shepherd Dog varies in color, and most colors are permissible. Strong rich colors are preferred. Nose black. Pale, washed-out colors and blues or livers are serious faults. A white dog or a dog with a nose that is not predominantly black, must be disqualified.

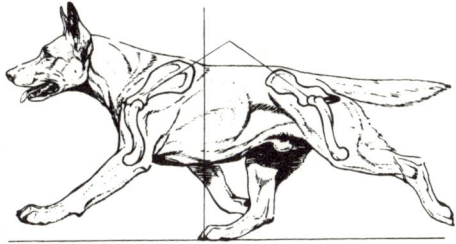

A balanced, extended trot.

COAT: The ideal dog has a double coat of medium length. The outer coat should be as dense as possible, hair straight, harsh and lying close to the body,. A slightly wavy outer coat, often of wiry texture, is permissible. The head, including the inner ear and foreface, and the legs and paws are covered with short hair, and the neck with longer and thicker hair. The rear of the forelegs and hind legs has somewhat longer hair extending to the pastern and hock, respectively. Faults in coat include soft, silky, too long outer coat, woolly, curly, and open coat.

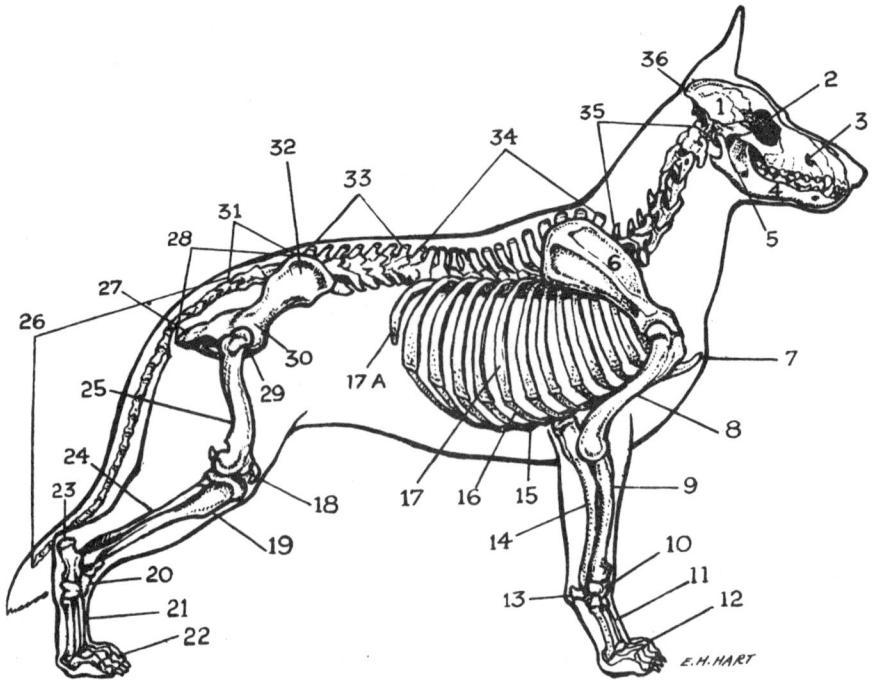

SKELETON OF A GERMAN SHEPHERD DOG

1. Cranium (skull). 2. Orbital cavity. 3. Nasal bone. 4. Mandible (jaw bone). 5. Condyle. 6. Scapula (shoulder blade, including spine and acromion process of scapula). 7. Prosternum. 8. Humerus (upper arm). 9. Radius (front forearm bone —see Ulna). 10. Carpus (pastern joint. Comprising seven bones). 11. Metacarpus (pastern. Comprising five bones). 12. Phalanges (digits or toes). 13. Pisiform (accessory carpal bone). 14. Ulna. 15. Sternum. 16. Costal cartilage (lower, cartilaginous section of ribs). 17. Rib bones. 17a. Floating rib (not connected by costal cartilage to sternum). 18. Patella (knee joint). 19. Tibia (with fibula comprises shank bone). 20. Tarsus (comprising seven bones. 21. Metatarsus (comprising five bones). 22. Phalanges (toes or digits of hind foot). 23. Os calcis (point of hock). 24. Fibula. 25. Femur (thigh bone). 26. Coccygeal vertebra (bones of tail. Number varies—18 to 23 normal). 27 Pubis. 28. Pelvic bone entire (pubis, ilium, ischium). 29. Head of femur. 30. Ischium. 31. Sacral vertebra (comprising five fused vertebra). 32. Ilium. 33. Lumbar vertebra. 34. Thoracic vertebra (dorsal, with spinal process or withers). 35. Cervical vertebra (bones of the neck). 36. Occipit.

The intelligence of the breed is demonstrated through its facial expression.